Rhythms for
Busy People

A pocket companion

Ray Simpson

From the Community of Aidan and Hilda

**kevin
mayhew**

First published in 2005 by

KEVIN MAYHEW LTD
Buxhall, Stowmarket, Suffolk, IP14 3BW
E-mail: info@kevinmayhewltd.com

9 8 7 6 5 4 3 2 1 0

ISBN 1 84417 357 7
Catalogue No. 1500775

Cover design by Angela Selfe
Edited by Marian Reid
Typesetting by Richard Weaver

Printed and bound in Great Britain

Dedication

I dedicate this book to Ian Nicholson and Christians in movements such as 24-7, boiler houses and YMAM who are waking us up to the fact that the Western Christian scene can be quite parochial: that a new wave of mobility is needed which takes prayer rhythms out of the boxes and into the byeways and highways of the twenty-first-century.

Also by Ray Simpson:

Celtic Daily Light: a spiritual journey throughout the year
Church of the Isles: a prophetic strategy for renewal
Exploring Celtic Spirituality: historic roots for our future
A Pilgrim Way: a new Celtic monasticism for everyday people

The Celtic Prayer Book is published in four volumes:

Volume One
Prayer Rhythms: fourfold patterns for each day and season

Volume Two
Saints of the Isles: a year of feasts

Volume Three
*Healing the Land: natural seasons, sacraments and special
services*

Volume Four
Great Celtic Christians: alternative worship

About the author

Ray Simpson is a co-founder of the worldwide Community
of Aidan and Hilda and is its first guardian. He is a priest
and pastor in the Christian Church, and a well-known
author. He lives on The Holy Island of Lindisfarne, near to
the Community's Retreat and Guest House, The Open
Gate, Holy Island, Berwick-Upon-Tweed, TD15 2SD UK.

CONTENTS

CONTENTS

INTRODUCTION

The first volume of the Celtic Prayer Book series, *Prayer Rhythms: fourfold patterns for each day*, was published in 2003, and was well received. It also inspired musicians to record accompanying music and has begun to be used in churches and groups. Most people in our mobile, multi-choice society, however, cannot be in churches or groups at set times. They may be travelling or moving from one task to another. To meet this need we have produced a pocket edition for busy people. This includes Morning, Midday, Evening and Night Prayer for each day of the week, omitting the seasonal material. This edition also incorporates Bible readings for each service, which are printed in full. These include a psalm, Old Testament and New Testament reading for each Morning and Evening Prayer. In addition, the Community of Aidan and Hilda's basic everyday prayers, designed to be memorised, are included for the first time.

This pocket companion can be used as a personal breviary, by groups, or as part of a service, and so prayers are divided between voices – Leader or Reader, and All. Responses or prayers for All, therefore, are in bold type.

Christians, Jews and Muslims have the great idea of reflecting the rhythm of the sun in their prayers – its rising, zenith and setting. This book helps busy people do this, too. These prayer rhythms can accompany us to work or leisure. Any of the prayers which are memorised can be said while driving, jogging or cooking, walking, queuing or sitting at a desk.

We hope that this handy book, which can be kept in

a pocket, handbag, car glove compartment or workplace
drawer, will become a familiar and much-loved companion
to many.

Jesus the Traveller

In taking prayer rhythms out of churches and into everyday life we are echoing Jesus himself. This person, who
Christians believe is the Son of God, and who most people
in the world respect as a prophet, travelled all his life in
one way or another.

It started in his mother Mary's womb. She and her
partner had to travel in order to register their names in
person for a census. So the unborn Jesus had a bumpy ride
on a donkey as they travelled to Bethlehem, in Palestine.
After Jesus was born, the jealous local ruler, hearing what
a draw Jesus was, ordered all the newly-born boys in that
area to be killed. Jesus' parents were guided by a dream to
escape. They became asylum seekers in Egypt. If you go to
Egypt today, you can follow the route people say they
took, and see the sites of friendly pagan communities who
gave them shelter and food.

When it became safe to return to their home country,
Jesus' parents set up home in a town called Nazareth. There
Jesus was an apprentice in his father's carpenter shop.
Nazareth was near the great trade routes. Large convoys
of travellers passed by with goods to buy, sell or export.
Jesus probably befriended some of them as they chatted to
him in the workshop. At the age of twelve, Jesus' parents
took him to the big city, Jerusalem. On their way back with
a large company of travellers, they realised that Jesus was
missing. They went back and found Jesus asking some

learned people questions in order to gain wisdom. 'Why did you go missing?' his parents asked him. Jesus told them, in effect, 'I have my own journey to make, and I have an Inner Guide who is as close to me as my earthly father.'

At the age of thirty, after his father had died, Jesus left behind his home ties. He travelled north to a rural inland sea named Galilee, got to know the area, and spent time alone in meditation. He intuited a divine call, and was to invite certain people to travel with him. The first two were fisherfolk. 'Leave behind your fishing nets and your income and follow me,' he told them. Something about Jesus made them want to do this. Twelve working people followed him full-time.

Sometimes his fellow travellers became worried about material things. Jesus advised them to learn from nature. 'The wild flowers do not work but God clothes them with a beauty greater than that of a superstar,' he reminded them. 'If God provides for flowers and birds, how much more will God look after you?'

Jesus was a free spirit. He had something that some leaders of political and religious organisations lacked: an inner authority. Crowds flocked to listen to him in the outdoors. He told them that every human being could choose to travel with him and be free, or to stay stuck to possessions and ego trips, which led to a dead end.

Sometimes even his closest fellow travellers had doubts. 'How can we know the road to travel?' asked one traveller named Thomas. Jesus replied, 'I myself am the Road. You can be wherever I am.' At that time Thomas and his friends did not understand what Jesus meant. People who were tied to power games and ego trips tried to smear Jesus and have him falsely accused. They succeeded and Jesus was executed between two thieves.

What was the point of being a Traveller now? His mother and his closest friends, male and female, followed his body to the tomb and anointed it with spices. But life seemed to be at a full stop – albeit with a question mark at the back of their minds.

Two days after Jesus' death a couple of his friends were walking the seven miles from his burial place to their village, talking about the splits and disappointments among Jesus' followers. A third person caught up with them, walked beside them, and joined in the conversation. As they walked and talked, they experienced a burning sensation inside. When they reached their house they invited the stranger in to share a simple meal. As the stranger broke the bread, they realised he did this in exactly the way Jesus always broke bread. Suddenly, they KNEW this man was, in fact, Jesus.

'I am still alive, still travelling,' Jesus said. 'Travel back to Jerusalem and tell them there that I am alive.' They travelled back, and to their amazement learned that others had also met Jesus.

Jesus stayed around, on and off, in a different form to the body he had before his death, but so that they could touch him, eat and talk with him, for six weeks. Before the six weeks ended, Jesus took them up a mountain: 'I will always be with you, to the end of time,' he assured them. 'So keep on travelling. Get out there, go to people in every corner of the world, in every part of life, and immerse them in the divine presence.' This they did, which is why the first followers of Jesus after his death and resurrection were known as followers of the Way.

As the centuries have gone by, there have been Christians who have turned a movement into a monu-ment, and who have put acquiring things above travelling.

But some have always kept on travelling with Jesus – more than we might think, since they do not grab the headlines.

This book keeps the spirit of 'Jesus the Traveller' alive. It comes from the international Community of Aidan and Hilda, which calls people to become Explorers and then Voyagers of Jesus' Way.

Note to the Reader

Psalms and other Bible readings are printed out for each service for the ease of the user. There is, however, nothing to stop you using a lectionary and a Bible as well.

The main churches provide The Revised Common Lectionary of Bible Readings for Morning and Evening Prayer each day.

Celtic Daily Light and *Saints of the Isles* (Volume 2 of The Celtic Prayer Book series) both include a daily Bible lectionary.

SUNDAY – NEW LIFE

In Jewish tradition Sunday is an image of the first day of
creation. Jesus Christ, Son of God, rose from the dead on
the first day of the week, so for Christians Sunday is a day
to celebrate resurrection and new life.

SUNDAY MORNING PRAYER

Rising from death, today Christ greets his people.
Rising with all creation, we greet him as our King.

or

Shine on us, O God, like the sun that lights up day.
Chase away the dark and all shadow of sin.
We will rejoice and be glad in you.

Thanksgiving
There may be singing
Psalm 24 may be read as follows

The earth belongs to God,
as do all things and people who live on it.

Out of the fluid cosmos God created its firmness.

Who may ascend to the high dwelling of God?

**Whoever is clean of heart
and whoever does not cling to what is false
will receive the Almighty's blessing
and the Saviour's embrace.
Such are those who seek the face of our forebears' God.**

**Open up the gates
that the King of glory may come in.**

Who is the King of glory?

**The Immortal God, mighty and strong,
is the King of glory.**

**Open up the gates
that the King of glory may come in.**

Who is the King of glory?

**The eternal and all-powerful God
is the King of glory.**

Let us recollect the presence of the Risen Christ
with us now.

Short silence

Forgiveness

The following or other words of confession and
forgiveness may be used

Christ Jesus, in the light of your risen presence,
and in union with your first frail apostles,
we say sorry:
For not weighing your words,
for not sharing your trials,
for not believing your promises.

O loving Christ, hanged on a tree yet risen
in the morning,
scatter the sin from our souls
as the mist from the hills.
Begin what we do, inform what we say,
redeem who we are.
In you we place our hope, now and for evermore.

God's Word (1)

Isaiah 60:1-3; 19-22

Arise, shine; for your light
has come,
and the glory of the Lord has risen upon you.
For darkness shall cover the earth,
and thick darkness the peoples;
but the Lord will arise upon you,
and his glory will appear over you.

15

Nations shall come to your light,
and kings to the brightness of your dawn.

The sun shall no longer be
your light by day,
nor for brightness shall the moon
give light to you by night;
but the Lord will be your everlasting light,
and your God will be your glory.
Your sun shall no more go down,
or your moon withdraw itself;
for the Lord will be your everlasting light,
and your days of mourning shall be ended.

Your people shall all be righteous;
they shall possess the land for ever.
They are the shoot that I planted, the work of my hands,
so that I might be glorified.
The least of them shall become a clan,
and the smallest one a mighty nation;
I am the Lord;
in its time I will accomplish it quickly.

There may be singing or silence

Proclamation

Jesus says: I am the resurrection and the life.

You break the power of sin and death.

I am the bread of life.

16

You feed and fill the hungry.

I am the true vine.

You bring us life eternal.

God's Word (2)

Colossians 3:9-17

Do not lie to one another, seeing that you have stripped off the old self with its practices and have clothed yourselves with the new self, which is being renewed in knowledge according to the image of its creator. In that renewal there is no longer Greek and Jew, circumcised and uncircumised, barbarian, Scythian, slave and free; but Christ is all and in all!

As God's chosen ones, holy and beloved, clothe yourselves with compassion, kindness, humility, meekness, and patience. Bear with one another and, if anyone has a complaint against another, forgive each other; just as the Lord has forgiven you, so you also must forgive.

Above all, clothe yourselves with love, which binds everything together in perfect harmony. And let the peace of Christ rule in your hearts, to which indeed you were called in the one body. And be thankful. Let the word of Christ dwell in you richly; teach and admonish one another in all wisdom; and with gratitude in your hearts sing psalms, hymns, and spiritual songs to God. And whatever you do, in word or deed, do everything in the name of the Lord Jesus, giving thanks to God the Father through him.

The following may be said

We believe, O God of all gods,
that you are the eternal Maker of life.
We believe, O God of all gods,
that you are the eternal Maker of love.

We believe, O Ruler and God of all people,
that you are the Creator of the skies above,
that you are the Creator of the oceans below,
that you are the Creator of the eternal realms.

We believe, O Ruler and God of all people,
that you are the One who created our souls
and set their course;
that you are the One who created our bodies
from earth;
that you gave to our bodies their breath
and to our souls their possession.

God, bless to us our bodies.
God, bless to us our souls.
God, bless to us our living.
God, bless to us our goals.

Silence or singing

Intercession

Thank you for bringing us
to the beginning of this week.

Keep us from falling into sin.

Through the resurrection of your Son
you overcame the hold of sin and death.

Transform us in all our ways.

Risen Christ, bring newness of life
**Into our stale routines,
into our wearied spirits,
into our tarnished relationships.**

*The following themes may be used as headings
for extended intercessions*

We pray for believers.
May their lives be signs of joyful service.

We pray for our churches.
**May they bring honour to you,
and healing to the people.**

We pray for people in authority.
May they strive for justice and peace.

We pray for our local communities.
**May this be a day of refreshment for traders
and all who live and work in our local communities.**

We pray for our homes.
May they be places of hospitality and hope.

There may be singing

Now may we know your presence
as we enjoy the company of others.

**The God of life go with us,
the Risen Christ beside us,
the vibrant Spirit within us.**

SUNDAY MIDDAY PRAYER

*This may be said before or after a meal and Alleluias may be
sung.*

In a longer Midday Prayer, Psalm 67 may be said as follows

God, be gracious to us and bless us.
May your face shine upon us.

**Make known your ways on earth,
your saving health among all nations.**

May all the peoples praise you, O God.
May all the peoples praise you.

**May the nations be glad and sing for joy,
for you rule the peoples justly
and guide the nations upon earth.**

May all the peoples praise you, O God.
May all the peoples praise you.

**Then the land will yield its produce
and our God will bless us.**

You will bless us,
and the ends of the earth will honour you.

You give us well-being in the midst of the day.

**A day of renewal;
a day of growth;
a day of sharing food.**

You were with us at the breaking of the day.
Be with us in the breaking of bread.

*A candle may be lit
One of the following may be said*

I would prepare a feast and be host
to the great High King,
with all the company of heaven.
The nourishment of pure love be in my house,
and the roots of repentance.
May we have baskets of love to give,
with cups of mercy for everybody.
Sweet Jesus, be here with us,
with all the company of heaven.
May this meal be full of cheerfulness,
for this is a feast of the great High King,
who is our host for all eternity.

Attributed to St Brigid

or

May the freshness and the fragrance of the farms
be with us as we eat.
May the freshness and fragrance of Christ
be with us as we meet.

or

The food which we are to eat
is earth, water and sun,
coming to us through pleasing plants.
The food which we are to eat
is the fruit of the labour of many creatures.
We are thankful for it.
May it give us health, strength, joy,
and may it increase our love.

or

**Risen Christ of the miraculous catching of fish
and the perfect lakeside meal,
be with us as we share this food.**

or

**Generous God,
as once you multiplied the five loaves and two fishes,
multiply the gifts each of us brings,
that from our sharing together blessings may flow.**

SUNDAY EVENING PRAYER

Spirit of the Risen Christ,
as the lamps light up the evening,
shine into our hearts and kindle in us
the fire of your love.

Candles may be lit
These words may be said or sung

The light of Christ has come into the world.

The light of Christ has come into the world.

The following is said or sung

Light of the world, in grace and beauty,
mirror of God's eternal face,
transparent flame of love's free duty,
you bring salvation to our race.
Now, as we see the lights of evening,
we raise our voice in hymns of praise.
Worthy are you of endless blessing,
sun of our night, lamp of our days.

Psalm

I keep the Lord always before me.

Because you are at my right hand,
I shall not be moved.

I keep the Lord always before me.

**Therefore my heart is glad, and my soul rejoices;
my body also rests secure.**

I keep the Lord always before me.

**For you do not give me up to destruction,
or let your faithful one see the Pit.**

I keep the Lord always before me.

**You show me the path of life.
In your presence there is fullness of joy.**

I keep the Lord always before me.

In your right hand are pleasures for evermore.

Psalm 16:8-11

This may be followed by silence

We offer to you, Lord, the troubles of this day;
we lay down our burdens at your feet.
Forgive us our sins, give us your peace,
and help us to receive your Word.

In the name of Christ. Amen.

God's Word (1)

Isaiah 44:1-8.

But now hear, O Jacob my servant,
Israel whom I have chosen!
Thus says the Lord who made you,
who formed you in the womb and will help you:
Do not fear, O Jacob my servant,
Jeshurun whom I have chosen.
For I will pour water on the thirsty land,
and streams on the dry ground;
I will pour my spirit upon your descendants,
and my blessing on your offspring.
They shall spring up like a green tamarisk,
like willows by flowing streams.
This one will say, 'I am the Lord's',
another will be called by the name of Jacob,
yet another will write on the hand,
'The Lord's', and adopt the name of Israel.

Thus says the Lord, the King of Israel
and his Redeemer, the Lord of hosts:
I am the first and I am the last;
besides me there is no god.
Who is like me? Let them proclaim it,
let them declare and set it forth before me.
Who has announced from of old the things to come?
Let them tell us what is yet to be.
Do not fear, or be afraid;
have I not told you from of old and declared it?
You are my witnesses!
Is there any god besides me?
There is no other rock; I know not one.

This is the Word of the Lord.
Thanks be to God.

Thanksgiving

There may be singing

We give you thanks, our Provider,
that you are always present,
in all things, each day and each night.
We give you thanks for your gifts of creation,
life and friendship.
We give you thanks for the particular blessings
of this day.

There may be a brief pause. Blessings may be named

God's Word (2)

2 Timothy 2:8-13

Remember Jesus Christ, raised from the dead, a descendant of David – that is my gospel, for which I suffer hardship, even to the point of being chained like a criminal. But the word of God is not chained. Therefore I endure everything for the sake of the elect, so that they may also obtain the salvation that is in Christ Jesus, with eternal glory. The saying is sure:

If we have died with him, we will also live with him;
if we endure, we will also reign with him;
if we deny him, he will also deny us;
if we are faithless, he remains faithful –
for he cannot deny himself.

There may be silent reflection or singing

Intercession

In the following intercessions there may be free prayer where indicated (. . .)

Into your hands, O Lord,
we place our families,
our neighbours,
our brothers and sisters in Christ,
and all whom we have met today (. . .)

Enfold them in your will.

Into your hands, O Lord,
we place all who are victims of prejudice,
oppression or neglect; the frail, the unwanted (. . .)

**May everyone be cherished
from conception to the grave.**

Into your hands, O Lord,
we place all who are restless,
sick, or prey to the powers of evil (. . .)

Keep guard over them.

Risen Christ,
bring renewal to the land and to the Church,
to ordained ministries and to religious communities.

**Raise up new callings and communities
that meet the need of our times.**

There may be singing

Lord Jesus Christ, Light of the world,
by your cross you have overcome all darkness
that oppresses.
Come and shine on us here in (. . .)
That we may grow and live together in your love
which makes us one with all humanity.

**The grace of our Lord Jesus Christ,
the love of God,
and the fellowship of the Holy Spirit
be with us all evermore. Amen.**

Bring us to our resurrection without end.

SUNDAY NIGHT PRAYER

A candle symbolising the Risen Christ is lit

Christ, rising in glory, scatters the darkness
from our hearts.

**Glory to you, Christ our King,
radiant with light,
morning and night give thanks and praise.**

Psalm 126

When the Lord restored the fortunes of Zion,
we were like those who dream.
Then our mouth was filled with laughter,
and our tongue with shouts of joy;
then it was said among the nations,
'The Lord has done great things for them.'
The Lord has done great things for us,
and we rejoiced.

Restore our fortunes, O Lord,
like the watercourses in the Negeb.
May those who sow in tears
reap with shouts of joy.
Those who go out weeping,
bearing the seed for sowing,
shall come home with shouts of joy,
carrying their sheaves.

There may be singing

Lord Jesus Christ, who at this hour lay in the tomb
and so hallowed the grave to be a bed of hope,
may we lie down in hope and rise up with you.

We need no longer fear death,
For by your death you have destroyed death.
We need not lie down in anger,
For your love has triumphed over hate.

29

We need not sleep as those without hope,
**For by your rising life you bring hope
and life eternal.**

Into our place of darkness,
into our place of strife,
into our fears and worries,
Come with your risen life.

Into those who are dying,
into those weary of life,
into those tired from exertions,
Come with your risen life.

Renew us this night, Lord, in body and soul,
that waking or sleeping we may know your presence
with us.

God's Word

John 20:19-21

*When it was evening on that day, the first day of the week, and
the doors of the house where the disciples had met were locked
for fear of the Jews, Jesus came and stood among them and said,
'Peace be with you.' After he said this, he showed them his hands
and his side. Then the disciples rejoiced when they saw the Lord.
Jesus said to them again, 'Peace be with you. As the Father has
sent me, so I send you.'*

This night, O Victor over death,
raise me from the death of denial;
raise me from the death of fear,
raise me from the death of despair.

**This night, O Victor over death,
wake me to the eternal 'Yes';
wake me to the rays of Hope;
wake me to the light of Dawn.**

There may be singing

The stone that sealed the tomb
has been rolled away.
**Christ is no longer among the dead,
he is here with us.**

We pray that the stones will roll away from those
who are trapped in deathly places. . .

Examples may be mentioned (. . .)

Our loved ones bless and keep, O God,
wherever they are (. . .)

Loved ones may be named

There may be silence

We lie down in peace,
knowing our sins are forgiven.
**We lie down in peace,
knowing death has no fear.**

We lie down in peace,
knowing no powers can harm us.
**We lie down in peace,
knowing angels are near.**

**Deep peace of the setting sun,
deep peace of the forgiving heart,
deep peace of the risen Christ,
be ours, tonight, for ever.**

You fell asleep in mortal flesh,
O Lord and Leader,
but on the third day you rose again.
Now you watch over us as we sleep,
you restore our souls and preserve our life.
In love of you we will take our rest.

In love of you we will take our rest.

Great God,
as you brought Christ
safely through the night of sin and death
to his rising at dawn,
so bring us through this night
that we may offer you our prayers at dawn
and walk in the light eternal.

MONDAY – CREATION

Since Sunday, the first day of the week, was set aside as a day of rest as well as a celebration of Christ's resurrection, we use Monday, the first day of the working week, to focus on creation, the earth, and the creative activities of humans, who are co-creators with God.

MONDAY MORNING PRAYER

God of life, you summon the day to dawn
and call us to create with you.

You are the Rock from which all earth is fashioned.
You are the Food from which all souls are fed.
You are the Force from which all powerlines travel.
You are the Source who is creation's head.

Thanksgiving

There may be singing

Psalm

Creator God, how great you are!
You clothe yourself in light,
you stretch out the skies like a tent.

Winds are your messengers,
flames are your servants.
You water the earth until it gives us food.

How abundant are your works, O God.
In wisdom have you made them all.

The creatures teeming the earth,
the sea, vast and wide;
innumerable things, small and great, live within it –
all these look to you for their food in due season.
When you send forth your Spirit they are created
and you renew the face of the earth.

May your glory last for ever.
May you always have joy in what you have created.

May our thoughts always give you pleasure.
May we always rejoice in you.

Psalm 104

God's Word (1)

Isaiah 55:6-13

Seek the Lord while he may be found,
call upon him while he is near;
let the wicked forsake their way,
and the unrighteous their thoughts;
let them return to the Lord, that he may have mercy on them,
and to our God, for he will abundantly pardon.

For my thoughts are not your thoughts,
nor are your ways my ways, says the Lord.
For as the heavens are higher than the earth,
so are my ways higher than your ways
and my thoughts higher than your thoughts.

For as the rain and the snow come down from heaven,
and do not return there until they have watered the earth,
making it bring forth and sprout,
giving seed to the sower and bread to the eater,
so shall my word be that goes out from my mouth;
it shall not return to me empty,
but it shall accomplish that which I purpose,
and succeed in the thing for which I sent it.

For you shall go out in joy,
and be led back in peace;
the mountains and the hills before you
shall burst into song,
and all the trees of the field shall clap their hands.
Instead of the thorn shall come up the cypress;
instead of the brier shall come up the myrtle;
and it shall be to the Lord for a memorial,
for an everlasting sign that shall not be cut off.

The Glory of Creation

For earth and sea and sky in the harmony of colour,
We give you thanks, O God.

For the air of the eternal seeping through the physical,

We give you thanks, O God.

For the everlasting glory dipping into time,

We give you thanks, O God.

For nature resplendent, growing beasts,
emergent crops, singing birds, the energies of the city,

We give you thanks, O God.

For the Person you sent to restore us when we
fell away from the goodness of your creation,

We give you thanks, O God.

For harmony restored through your Spirit
moving upon the turbulent waters of our lives,

We give you thanks, O God.

For the honour you give us
of lives flowing in the rhythm of your tides,

We give you thanks, O God.

For setting each of us, like the stars upon their courses,
within the orbit of your love,

We give you thanks, O God.

God's Word (2)

Acts 14:8-17

*In Lystra there was a man sitting who could not use his feet and
had never walked, for he had been crippled from birth. He listened
to Paul as he was speaking. And Paul, looking at him intently
and seeing that he had faith to be healed, said in a loud voice,
'Stand upright on your feet.' And the man sprang up and began*

*to walk. When the crowds saw what Paul had done, they shouted
in the Lycaonian language, 'The gods have come down to us in
human form!' Barnabas they called Zeus, and Paul they called
Hermes, because he was the chief speaker. The priest of Zeus,
whose temple was just outside the city, brought oxen and
garlands to the gates; he and the crowds wanted to offer sacri-
fice. When the apostles Barnabas and Paul heard of it, they tore
their clothes and rushed out into the crowd, shouting, 'Friends,
why are you doing this? We are mortals just like you, and we
bring you good news, that you should turn from these worthless
things to the living God, who made the heaven and the earth and
the sea and all that is in them. In past generations he allowed all
the nations to follow their own ways; yet he has not left himself
without a witness in doing good – giving you rains from heaven
and fruitful seasons, and filling you with food and your hearts
with joy.'*

I believe, O God of all gods,
that you are the eternal Creator of life.
I believe, O God of all gods,
that you are the eternal Father of love.
I believe, O Lord and God of the peoples,
that you are the Creator of the high heavens.
I believe, O Lord and God of the peoples,
that you created my soul and set its warp.

Forgiveness

**Creator and Saviour,
we have exploited earth for our selfish ends,
turned our backs on the cycles of life
and forgotten we are your stewards.
Now soils become barren,
air and water become unclean,
species disappear,
aIn penitence we come to you.**

There may be silence

God, have mercy.
Christ, have mercy.
God, have mercy.

This may be followed by meditation or singing

Intercession

One or more of the following prayers may be said

This we know, the earth does not belong to us.
The earth is God's and we will serve it.
This we know, we did not weave the web of life.
The earth is God's and we will serve it.
Whatever befalls the earth
befalls the sons and daughters of the earth.
The earth is God's and we will serve it.

Caring Father God,
we offer to you the fuels and forests,
the seas and soil, the air and animals.

**May we steward your creation to your glory
and for the benefit of future generations.**

Bless all work done today
that enables the human family
to be clothed, fed and housed,
to travel and learn,
to communicate and exchange wisely,
to craft and celebrate,
in everything reflecting your glory.

Worker Christ, as we enter our workplace,
may we bring your presence with us.
Grace us to speak your peace and perfect order
into its atmosphere.
Remind us to acknowledge your authority
over all that will be thought, decided and
accomplished within it.
Give us a fresh supply of truth and beauty
on which to draw as we work.

In dependence on the God of life
may we cherish the precious earth:
the earth of the God of life,
the earth of the Christ of love,
the earth of the Spirit Holy.
In dependence on the God of Life
may our life this day have blessing:

the blessing of the God of life,
the blessing of the Christ of love
the blessing of the Spirit Holy.

There may be singing

God bless the sky that is above us,
the earth that is beneath us,
your image deep within us,
the day that lies before us.

MONDAY MIDDAY PRAYER

Great Spirit,
whose breath is felt in the soft breeze,
and whose life surges through socket and screen,
we seek your strength in the midst of the day.
May we, and the peoples of the world,
work in dignity and walk in the beauty of the day.

Blessed be God the birther of life.
Blessed be God the giver of light.
Blessed be God the bestower of skills.

If God had not supported us,
evildoers would have swallowed us up,
the flood would have engulfed us,
the raging waters would have swept us away.
Praise God that we have escaped like a bird
freed from a trap.

Truly our help is in God,
Maker of heaven and earth.
Psalm 124

O Son of God, change my heart.
Your Spirit composes the songs of the birds
and the buzz of the bees.
Your creation is a million wondrous miracles,
beautiful to look upon,
I ask of you just one more miracle:
beautify my soul.

O God, you called all life into being,
your presence is around us now,
your Spirit enlivens all who work.
May your kingdom come on earth.

Impart to us wisdom to understand your ways,
to manage well the tasks of this day.
Make us co-creators with you,
so that when day fades
we may come to you without shame.

You will labour, but God will bless your work.
You will walk, but God will bless your footsteps.
You will suffer, but God will bless your tears.

Contained in the earth are the seeds of all.
Contained in the soul is the Son of God.

Listen to the words of Christ:
Happy you who are gentle –
the earth belongs to you.

**We pray for this world you have given us,
for the planting of seeds
and for the propagation of stock
in the soils and commerce of the world.**

Encircle those who can neither sow nor reap
because human ills have drained them.
Give us wisdom to manage technology
for the world's good.
Sustain those who eke out the minerals,
create textiles, grow crops or rear cattle.

There may be singing or free prayer

Good God, be with us in every experience of life.
When we neglect you

Remind us of your presence.

When we are frightened

Give us courage.

When we are tempted

Give us the power to resist.

When we are anxious and worried

Give us peace.

When we are weary in service

Renew our tired frame.

There may be singing

God who dances with creation,
plants your likeness in the people,
and strikes the world with thunder,
send us out to fill the world with love.

MONDAY EVENING PRAYER

We bless you, O God, and forget not
all your benefits.

**We bless you for your creation
which is alive with your glory.**

You nod and beckon to us
through every stone and star.

**As the sun sets in the west
so we settle down with you.**

*There may be silent reflection on the
spoiling of God's creation, or singing*

Psalm

The mighty God calls to the earth
from the sun's rising to its sleep.
God the Eternal Source shines forth
perfect in spiritual beauty.

**With fiery skies and raging storms
God calls to heaven, to earth:
'Bring to me those faithful souls
who give their hearts to me.'**

The Mighty God requires our eyes
and beckons us to listen.
'You cannot earn a place near me,
for all that lives is mine:

**The cattle on a thousand hills,
the wildlife, trees and birds.
If I hungered, I'd not tell you,
for all that lives is mine.**

So call to me in trial, in joy,
and give to me your thanks.
Do not ingratiate yourselves,
let gratitude abound.'
From Psalm 50

We bless you, Lord,

For the beauty of the trees,
the softness of the air,
the fragrance of the grass.

We bless you, Lord,

For the soaring of the skies,
the rhythms of the earth,
the stillness of the night.

We bless you, Lord,

For the twinkling of the stars,
the freshness of the morning,
the dewdrops on the flower.

44

We bless you, Lord,

For the taste of good food,
the trail of the sun,
and the life that never goes away.

Chief Dan George

God's Word (1)

Isaiah 24:4-5

> *The earth dries up and withers,*
> *the world languishes and withers;*
> *the heavens languish together with the earth.*
> *The earth lies polluted*
> *under its inhabitants;*
> *for they have transgressed laws,*
> *violated the statutes,*
> *broken the everlasting covenant.*

Silence

You Are My Island

Lord, you are my island;

In your bosom I nest.

You are the calm of the sea;

In that peace I rest.

You are the waves on the shore's
glistening stones;

Their sound is my hymn.

You are the song of the birds;

Their tune I sing.

You are the sea breaking on rock;

I praise you with the swell.

You are the ocean that laps my being;

In you I dwell.

God's Word (2)

Matthew 6:25-34

'Therefore I tell you, do not worry about your life, what you will eat or what you will drink, or about your body, what you will wear. Is not life more than food, and the body more than clothing? Look at the birds of the air; they neither sow nor reap nor gather into barns, and yet your heavenly Father feeds them. Are you not of more value than they? And can any of you by worrying add a single hour to your span of life? And why do you worry about clothing? Consider the lilies of the field, how they grow; they neither toil nor spin, yet I tell you, even Solomon in all his glory was not clothed like one of these. But if God so clothes the grass of the field, which is alive today and tomorrow is thrown into the oven, will he not much more clothe you — you of little faith? Therefore do not worry, saying, "What will we eat?" or "What will we drink?" or "What will we wear?" For it is the Gentiles who strive for all these things; and indeed your heavenly Father knows that you need all these things. But strive first for the kingdom of God and his righteousness, and all these things will be given to you as well.

'So do not worry about tomorrow, for tomorrow will bring worries of its own. Today's trouble is enough for today.'

I believe, O God of all gods,
that you are the eternal Creator of life.
I believe, O God of all gods,
that you are the eternal Father of love.
I believe, O Ruler and God of the peoples,
that you are the Creator of all that is.
I believe, O Ruler and God of the peoples,
that you created my soul and set its warp.

There may be meditation and singing

Thanksgiving

We give thanks for moments of grace
in the life of the cosmos:
for the explosion of a star and the birth of our planet.

**We give thanks for the moments of grace
in the life of a person;
the power of attraction and the wonder of a birth.**

Intercession

Generosity of God, spilling over into creation,
we bless you for flowers and their wealth of beauty,
for creatures and their glorious variety,
for seas and seasons and scents.
May we, too, reflect something of your glorious
    generosity.

47

We pray for the well-being of creation,
the healthfulness of the air,
the richness of the earth and its provisions,
and the beauty of the whole world.

Creator, make us co-workers with you
so that the earth and all who live upon it
may reap a full harvest.
Show us how to reflect your rhythms in our life and work,
and to conserve the world's rich resources.

Help us to give all creatures their due respect,
to tend cattle and crops with care.
Guide science along wise and considerate ways
that we may fashion agriculture that truly
enhances and that we may sustain a
vibrant environment.

Creator God, graciously hear us.

Peace to the land and all that grows on it.
Peace to the sea and all that swims in it.
Peace to the air and all that flies through it.
Peace with our God who calls us to serve.

The Creator who brought order out of chaos
give peace to us.
The Saviour who calmed the raging sea
give peace to us.
The Spirit who broods upon the deeps
give peace to us.

MONDAY NIGHT PRAYER

Let the light fade and the work be done.
Let the flowers and the desktops close.
Let the sun go down and the world become still,
and let the Son of God draw near.

Blessed be all creation,
And all that has life.

Blessed be the earth;
May it uplift our bed tonight.

Blest be the fire;
May it glow in us tonight.

Blest be the air;
May it make our night-breath sweet.

There may be singing

Psalm 104:1-4, 19-24

Bless the Lord, O my soul.
O Lord my God, you are very great.
You are clothed with honour and majesty,
wrapped in light as with a garment.
You stretch out the heavens like a tent,
you set the beams of your chambers on the waters,
you make the clouds your chariot,
you ride on the wings of the wind,
you make the winds your messengers,
fire and flame your ministers.

You have made the moon to mark the seasons;
the sun knows its time for setting.
You make darkness, and it is night,
when all the animals of the forest come creeping out.
The young lions roar for their prey,
seeking their food from God.
When the sun rises, they withdraw
and lie down in their dens.
People go out to their work
and to their labour until the evening.

O Lord, how manifold are your works!
In wisdom you have made them all;
the earth is full of your creatures.

We give you thanks that you are always present,
in all things, each day and each night.
We give you thanks for your gifts of creation,
life and friendship.
We give you thanks for the blessings of this day . . .

Blessings may be named in silence or aloud

When we are still we can sense you, our Maker,
we can feel your hand upon us.
All that has been made stirs within us
creation's song of praise.
Now we give you thanks for work completed.

We give you thanks for rest of night.

There may be silence or singing

Genesis 1:3-5, 31

Then God said, 'Let there be light'; and there was light. And God saw that the light was good; and God separated the light from the darkness. God called the light Day, and the darkness he called Night. And there was evening and there was morning, the first day.

God saw everything that he had made, and indeed, it was very good. And there was evening and there was morning, the sixth day.

Guardian of the planets,
kindler of the stars,
we pass into the darkness
encompassed by you.

We offer you our concerns
and the needs of your creation.

There may be silence or free prayer

Thank you for your love for us,
strong and nurturing.
We give back our lives to you.
Thank you for our minds and bodies.
We give back our lives to you.
Thank you for the past day.
We give back our lives to you.
After creation God rested.
We give back our lives to you.

Protect us through the hours of this night,
be they silent or stormy,
that we who are wearied by the changes
and chances of a restless world
may rest upon you eternally.

You created the world out of love.
Now we return to you in love.
Let us rest in God this night.
And awake in newness of life.

TUESDAY – PEACE: GOD WITH US

The peace for which we pray is not just the absence of war, but is rooted in the fundamental peacemaking action of God, who has made peace with the hostile human race by becoming one with it, having been made present in our world in human form. The incarnation of God's Son is an act of peacemaking that initiates a ceaseless peace process on earth. At his birth, angels proclaimed Jesus to be the Prince of Peace, and in the Celtic tradition Jesus is pictured as bounding down mountains towards human beings, holding out a hand of reconciliation. Jesus calls us, in turn, to become peacemakers.

TUESDAY MORNING PRAYER

Glory to the most High God
who has come to live among us.
He has come to make peace in a hostile world.

Christ, born of the loveliest Mary
You are with us in our birth.
Christ, brought up as a carpenter,
You are with us in our work.
Christ, friend of seeker and outcast,
You are with us in our friendships.
Christ, noble in suffering and death,
You are with us in our trials.

Christ, eternal Son of God,
You are with us evermore.

There may be singing

Psalm

You forgave the sins of your people
and restored your land, O God.

Restore us too, O God our Saviour.
Show us your unfailing love,
revive us again that we may rejoice in you.

I will listen to what the Eternal God,
who promises us divine peace, will say.

Your salvation is near those who reverence you,
so that your glory may dwell in our land.

Love and faithfulness meet together,
justice and peace embrace.

Faithfulness springs forth from the earth,
righteousness looks down from heaven.

The Eternal God will give us a harvest of goodness.

Righteousness prepares the way
for you to move among us.

From Psalm 85

Dear Son of Mary, you took flesh to redeem us,
change our hearts.

**Dear Son of God, you came to us with sacrificial love,
change our hearts.**

*There may be silence, spontaneous words of confession and these
words of forgiveness*

The Son of God bounds towards us
reaching out a hand of reconciliation.
Let us take it, and listen to God's Word.

God's Word (1)

Micah 4:1-4

*In days to come
the mountain of the Lord's house
shall be established as the highest of the mountains,
and shall be raised up above the hills.
Peoples shall stream to it,
and many nations shall come and say:
'Come, let us go up to the mountain of the Lord,
to the house of the God of Jacob;
that he may teach us his ways
and that we may walk in his paths.'
For out of Zion shall go forth instruction,
and the word of the Lord from Jerusalem.
He shall judge between many peoples,
and shall arbitrate between strong
    nations far away;*

they shall beat their swords into ploughshares,
and their spears into pruning-hooks;
nation shall not lift up sword against nation,
neither shall they learn war any more;
but they shall all sit under their own vines
*   and under their own fig trees,*
and no one shall make them afraid;
for the mouth of the Lord of hosts has spoken.

We Bless You, Lord

We bless you, great God of Israel,
For you have set your people free.

You have raised up for us a mighty Saviour,
Born of your servant David's family.

Through your holy prophets you promised of old
That you would save us from all who hate us.

You promised to show mercy to our forebears
And to remember your holy covenant.

You vowed to our ancestor Abraham
To set us free to worship you without fear.

The dawn from on high shall break upon us,
To shine on those in darkness and to guide us
**   into peace.**

Luke 1:68-79

God's Word (2)

Ephesians 2:12-22

Remember that you were at that time without Christ, being aliens from the commonwealth of Israel, and strangers to the covenants of promise, having no hope and without God in the world. But now in Christ Jesus you who once were far off have been brought near by the blood of Christ. For he is our peace; in his flesh he has made both groups into one and has broken down the dividing wall, that is, the hostility between us. He has abolished the law with its commandments and ordinances, so that he might create in himself one new humanity in place of the two, thus making peace, and might reconcile both groups to God in one body through the cross, thus putting to death that hostility through it. So he came and proclaimed peace to you who were far off and peace to those who were near; for through him both of us have access in one Spirit to the Father. So then you are no longer strangers and aliens, but you are citizens with the saints and also members of the household of God, built upon the foundation of the apostles and prophets, with Christ Jesus himself as the cornerstone. In him the whole structure is joined together and grows into a holy temple in the Lord; in whom you also are built together spiritually into a dwelling-place for God.

There may be meditation and singing

Intercession

Babe of heaven, defenceless Love,
you had to travel far from your home.

**Strengthen us on our pilgrimage of trust
on earth.**

King of glory, you accepted such humbling;
Clothe us with the garments of humility.

Your birth shows us the simplicity
of the Father's love;
Keep us in the simplicity of that love.

Your coming shows us the wonder of being human;
Help us to cherish every human life.

Child of Glory, Child of Mary,
at your birth you were proclaimed
the Prince of Peace.
You came to remove the wall that divides
one people from another.
May walls of hostility and fear
come tumbling down; especially (. . .)

Suggestions may be made

You call the peacemakers blessed.
Strengthen peacemakers in places torn apart
by the ravages of sin.

Suggestions may be made

Christ who comes with justice and peace,
we pray for the peace and well-being
of the whole world
and of all the churches.

We pray for victims of oppression and violence, especially
    (. . .)

There may be prepared or spontaneous intercessions,
silence, singing or the Lord's Prayer

God, direct our hours,
protect our assets,
still our hearts.
May we see the face of Christ
in everyone we meet.
May everyone we meet see the face of Christ in us.

Deep peace of the quiet earth to you.
Deep peace of the still air to you.
Deep peace of the forgiving heart to you.
Deep peace of the Son of peace.

TUESDAY MIDDAY PRAYER

There may be singing

In the whirling wheels of the world,
You are with us.
When the day takes its toll,
You are with us.
In the clamour of strife,
You are with us.

When the world turns sour,
You are with us.

Make us aware, dear God,
of the eye that beholds us,
the hand that holds us,
the heart that loves us,
the Presence that enfolds us.

Psalm 117

Praise the Lord, all you nations!
Extol him, all you peoples!
For great is his steadfast love towards us,
and the faithfulness of the Lord endures for ever.
Praise the Lord!

Glory to you, O God of life.
Glory to you, O Lord.

Jesus says:
Happy are you who are peacemakers;
you will be called God's children.

From Matthew 5:9

My peace I give to you,
not as the world gives do I give to you.

From John 14:27

There may be silence and singing

Circle us, O God, for the rest of the day.
Keep strife without,
keep peace within.

Circle us, O God, keep . . .

Suggestions may be made

Lead us from fear to trust.

Lead us from despair to hope.

Lead us from hate to love.

Lead us from war to peace.

Deep peace of the Son of peace,

Fill our hearts, our workplace, our world.

To be said or sung

**May the eternal Glory shine upon us,
may the Son of Mary stay beside us,
may the life-giving Spirit live always within us,
may the Three be with us for ever.**

TUESDAY EVENING PRAYER

The peace of Christ has come into the world.

The peace of Christ has come into the world.

*Mary's Song may be said or sung to the tune of 'Amazing
Grace'*

**Magnificat, magnificat!
Praise God, my soul, praise God.
The proud are downed,
the poor raised up.
Magnificat, my soul!**

Psalm

God is our refuge and strength,
a very present help in trouble.

**Therefore we will not fear,
though the earth should change,
though the mountains shake in the heart of the sea;
though its waters roar and foam,
though the mountains tremble with its tumult.**

There is a river whose streams
make glad the city of God,
the place where the Most High dwells.

**God is at the centre of the city
which therefore shall not be moved.
God will help it when the morning dawns.**

The nations are in uproar. Kingdoms totter.
God's voice thunders: the earth melts.

**The Lord of untold multitudes is with us;
the God of our founders is our refuge.**

Look carefully at the desolation
God is bringing about on the earth.
Everywhere wars are ceasing,
weapons are dismantled and destroyed
and God is saying:
'Be still and know that I am God!

I am exalted among the nations
I am exalted in the earth.'

The Lord of untold multitudes is with us;
The God of our founders is our refuge.

Psalm 46

Forgiveness

We offer to you, Lord, the troubles of this day;
we lay down our burdens at your feet.

There may be a pause

Forgive us our sins, give us your peace,
and help us to receive your Word.
In the name of Christ.

God's Word (1)

Isaiah 11:1-9

A shoot shall come out from the stock of Jesse,
and a branch shall grow out of his roots.
The spirit of the Lord shall rest on him,
the spirit of wisdom and understanding,
the spirit of counsel and might,
the spirit of knowledge and the fear of the Lord.
His delight shall be in the fear of the Lord.
He shall not judge by what his eyes see,
or decide by what his ears hear;

63

but with righteousness he shall judge the poor,
and decide with equity for the meek of the earth;
he shall strike the earth with the rod of his mouth,
and with the breath of his lips he shall kill the wicked.
Righteousness shall be the belt around his waist,
and faithfulness the belt around his loins.

The wolf shall live with the lamb,
the leopard shall lie down with the kid,
the calf and the lion and the fatling together,
and a little child shall lead them.
The cow and the bear shall graze,
their young shall lie down together;
and the lion shall eat straw like the ox.
The nursing child shall play over the hole of the asp,
and the weaned child shall put its hand on the adder's den.
They will not hurt or destroy
on all my holy mountain;
for the earth will be full of the knowledge of the Lord
as the waters cover the sea.

When the day takes its toll,
Christ bounds down the mountains towards us.
When we cry out in pain,
Christ bounds down the mountains towards us.
When all's well with the world,
Christ bounds down the mountains towards us.
When we need strength to do right,
Christ bounds down the mountains towards us.

God's Word (2)

Hebrews 1:1-6

Long ago God spoke to our ancestors in many and various ways by the prophets, but in these last days he has spoken to us by a Son, whom he appointed heir of all things; through whom he also created the worlds. He is the reflection of God's glory and the exact imprint of God's very being, and he sustains all things by his powerful word. When he had made purification for sins, he sat down at the right hand of the Majesty on high, having become as much superior to angels as the name he has inherited is more excellent than theirs.

For to which of the angels did God ever say, 'You are my Son; today I have begotten you'?
Or again, 'I will be his Father, and he will be my Son'? And again, when he brings the firstborn into the world, he says, 'Let all God's angels worship him.'

Thanksgiving

We give you thanks, our God,
that you are always present, in all things,
each day and each night.
We give you thanks for your gifts of creation,
life and friendship.
We give you thanks for the particular blessings
of this day . . .

There may be a brief pause,
the naming of blessings,
singing in tongues or a sung response

Intercession

Any of the following prayers may be used

Christ,
the peace of things above,
and the rest of those below,
establish in your peace the five continents,
and especially your universal Church.
Destroy wars from the ends of the earth
and disperse those who delight in terror.

Child of glory,
Child of Mary,
born in the stable,
King of all,
you came to our wasteland,
in our place suffered.
By choosing to be born as a child
you teach us to reverence every human life.
May we never despise, degrade or destroy life.
Rather, help us sustain and preserve it.

Child of Humanity,
Trinity's only Son,
gentle and strong
from whose line we come,
bring your peace to your warring children:

Peace between rich and poor,
peace between believers and unbelievers,
peace between parents and children.

Bring your peace to those we name before you now (. . .)

Persons may be named

There may be singing

Help us, Lord,
to guard our words,
to overcome hostility with love,
to make peace,
in love of the King of Life.

**Deep peace of the running wave be ours,
deep peace of the flowing air,
deep peace of the quiet earth,
deep peace of the shining stars,
deep peace of the Son of peace.**

TUESDAY NIGHT PRAYER

Peace to us and to all who seek good.

**The peace of the Spirit be mine this night;
the peace of the Son be mine this night;
the peace of the Father be mine this night;
the peace of all peace be mine this night;
each morning and evening of my life.**

There may be singing

We offer you, Lord, the troubles of this day;
we lay down our burdens at your feet.
Forgive us our sins,
give us your peace,
and help us to receive your Word.

Many people say, 'If only we might see some good!
Let some light from your face shine upon us, O God!'
You have put gladness in my heart
more than when all their material
benefits abound.
I will lie down and sleep in peace;
for you alone, O God, make me lie down in safety.

From Psalm 4

May fears of day recede.

May treasures of night draw near.

O Christ, Son of the living God,
may your holy angels guard our sleep,
may they watch over us as we rest
and hover around our beds.
Let them reveal to us in our dreams
visions of your glorious truth.
May no fears or worries delay
our willing, prompt repose.

The following or other words of Christ are read

Come to me, all you who are weary and burdened,
and I will give you rest. Take my yoke upon you
and learn from me, for I am gentle and humble of heart,
and you will find rest for your souls.

From Matthew 11: 28, 29

There may be meditation or sharing of thoughts

Our dear ones bless, O God,
and keep, wherever they are.

Dear ones may be named

**May Heaven's peacekeepers encircle us all
with their outstretched arms
to protect us from the hostile powers,
to put balm into our dreams,
to give us contented, sweet repose.**

We lie down in peace,
knowing our sins are forgiven.
**We lie down in peace,
knowing death has no fear.**
We lie down in peace,
knowing no powers can harm us.
**We lie down in peace,
knowing Jesus is near.**

Deep peace of the Son of Peace to you.

Say or sing to the tune 'Peace to You'

**Peace to you,
peace of his air flowing out to you.
Peace to you,
peace of his stars shining out to you.
Peace to you,
peace to you,
peace to you.**

WEDNESDAY – THE RENEWING, SENDING SPIRIT

In the middle of the week the focus is the God who sends and whose Spirit renews us and gives gifts for mission.

WEDNESDAY MORNING PRAYER

Come, Creator Spirit,
fresh as the morning dew,
Revive us and make us new.

Let us arise today in the Spirit's power:
In the place of fear,

God's strength to uphold me;

In the place of emptiness,

God's wisdom to guide me;

In the place of confusion,

God's eye for my seeing;

In the place of discord,

God's ear for my hearing;

In the place of froth,

God's word for my speaking;
to save me from false agendas
that harm my body or soul.

There may be singing

Psalm

Happy are those who heed neither the words
nor the ways of the godless,
whose delight is in God's law
on which they meditate day and night.

They are like trees planted by streams,
which yield their fruit every season.
Their leaves do not wither;
they flourish in all they do.

The godless are not so. They are like refuse
blown about by the wind.
They are like wrongdoers who fail to fool
a court of justice;
even if they sidle in with those who do right
they are exposed for what they are.
The way of the godless will come to nothing,
but God looks after the path of those who do right.

Glory to God, Creator, Redeemer,
Sustainer for ever. Amen.

Psalm 1

Forgiveness

From false desires and selfish deeds,

All-knowing God, deliver us.

From unworthy thoughts and prideful claims,

All-seeing God, deliver us.

From unclean hearts and petty ways,

All-cleansing God, deliver us.

God's Word (1)

Isaiah 49:1-8

Listen to me, O coastlands,
pay attention, you peoples from far away!
The Lord called me before I was born,
while I was in my mother's womb he named me.
He made my mouth like a sharp sword,
in the shadow of his hand he hid me;
he made me a polished arrow,
in his quiver he hid me away.
And he said to me, 'You are my servant,
Israel, in whom I will be glorified.'
But I said, 'I have laboured in vain,
I have spent my strength for nothing and vanity;
yet surely my cause is with the Lord,
and my reward with my God.'

And now the Lord says,
who formed me in the womb to be his servant,
to bring Jacob back to him,
and that Israel might be gathered to him,
for I am honoured in the sight of the Lord,
and my God has become my strength –
he says,
'It is too light a thing that you should be my servant
to raise up the tribes of Jacob
and to restore the survivors of Israel;
I will give you as a light to the nations,
that my salvation may reach to the end of the earth.'

Thus says the Lord,
the Redeemer of Israel and his Holy One,
to one deeply despised, abhorred by the nations,
the slave of rulers,
'Kings shall see and stand up,
princes, and they shall prostrate themselves,
because of the Lord who is faithful,
the Holy One of Israel, who has chosen you.'

Thus says the Lord:
In a time of favour I have answered you,
on a day of salvation I have helped you;
I have kept you and given you as a covenant to the people,
to establish the land,
to apportion the desolate heritages.

The Spirit Pours on Christ

The Immortal who bowed the heavens
bows his head before a mortal.

Glory!

The Uncreated enters the stream of created life.

Glory!

God becomes one with us,
and we are made one with God.

Glory!

Our lost innocence is restored
and the world is charged with the grandeur of God.

Glory!

74

Father love cascades over the Son;
the Spirit pours upon him.

God in Trinity is revealed.

Glory, glory, ever and everywhere!

God's Word (2)

Matthew 28:16-20

Now the eleven disciples went to Galilee, to the mountain to which Jesus had directed them. When they saw him, they worshipped him; but some doubted. And Jesus came and said to them, 'All authority in heaven and on earth has been given to me. Go therefore and make disciples of all nations, baptising them in the name of the Father and of the Son and of the Holy Spirit, and teaching them to obey everything that I have commanded you. And remember, I am with you always, to the end of the age.'

There may be meditation or singing

Intercession

Come like fire and warm our hearts.
Come like wind and refresh our frames.
Come like water and revive our souls.
Come like the earth and nourish our being.

**Holy Spirit, refine us,
that we may be just and true.
Sending Spirit, release us,
that we may touch lives for you.
Disturbing Spirit, re-charge us, wasted lives to renew.**

On those whose day is drab,

Come, Holy Spirit.

On those who harbour fear,

Come, Holy Spirit.

On a parched land,

Come, Holy Spirit.

There may be free prayer

Eternal God and Father,
you create us by your power
and redeem us by your love:
guide and strengthen us by your Spirit,
that we may give ourselves in love and service
to one another and to you.

There may be singing

May your church grow in holiness
and in numbers.

**Peace and blessing from the Spirit,
and from the Three who are ever One.**

76

WEDNESDAY MIDDAY PRAYER

Holy Spirit,
come as a gentle breeze
that cools in the heat of the day;
come as the calming Presence
that restores stillness to our being.

**Wind of Heaven,
blow away dross and deceits.
Refresh our battered souls.
Brace us for what is to come.**

There may be silence or singing

*Psalm 23 may be read in the following way.
A hymn version of this psalm may be sung*

*God is my shepherd,
who refreshes me in green pastures,
restores me by quiet waters,
and leads me to the right ways.*

With God I lack nothing I truly need.

*Even though I walk
through the valley of the shadow of death
I will fear no evil,
for you are with me, your protecting staff comforts me.*

With God I lack nothing I truly need.

You prepare a feast for me
even when hostile people surround me.
You anoint me with oil and my life overflows.

With God I lack nothing I truly need.

Surely goodness and mercy shall follow me all the days of
    my life
and I will dwell in your presence for ever.

Perfect Comforter! Wonderful Refreshment!
You make peace to dwell in our soul.
In our labour, you offer rest;
in temptation, strength.
From heaven shine forth with your glorious light.

From the Taizé Prayer Book

There may be silence or singing

When my life seems all duty and dust
in the midst of the day when we droop;
when routine things turn into rust
and people from valour do stoop;
then the Wild Goose comes to my aid:
her wings pass o'er and give shade,
make the day's scorching heat soon fade,
and I know in God's image I'm made
and that nothing of this world can degrade;
nothing of this world can degrade.

Andrew Dick

Happy are you when you are defamed
or excluded.
Leap for joy, your reward in heaven is great.   *(Matthew)*

The Spirit will show you what to say.   *(John)*

The Holy Spirit joins with our spirit
to affirm that we are children of God.   *(Paul)*

Alleluia!

There may be singing, sharing,
free prayer or the Lord's Prayer

Holy Spirit,
for the rest of the day renew in us:
Joy in our work,
life in our being,
love in our relationships.

WEDNESDAY EVENING PRAYER

Kindling Spirit, come;
inflame our waiting hearts.

Consoling Spirit, come;
you know our every need.

There may be singing

Psalm 139:1-12

O Lord, you have searched me and known me.
You know when I sit down and when I rise up;
you discern my thoughts from far away.
You search out my path and my lying down,
and are acquainted with all my ways.
Even before a word is on my tongue,
O Lord, you know it completely.
You hem me in, behind and before,
and lay your hand upon me.
Such knowledge is too wonderful for me;
it is so high that I cannot attain it.

Where can I go from your spirit?
Or where can I flee from your presence?
If I ascend to heaven, you are there;
if I make my bed in Sheol, you are there.
If I take the wings of the morning
and settle at the furthest limits of the sea,
even there your hand shall lead me,
and your right hand shall hold me fast.
If I say, 'Surely the darkness shall cover me,
and the light around me become night',
even the darkness is not dark to you;
the night is as bright as the day,
for darkness is as light to you.

There may be a pause

God's Word (1)

Jeremiah 31:31-34

The days are surely coming, says the Lord, when I will make a new covenant with the house of Israel and the house of Judah. It will not be like the covenant that I made with their ancestors when I took them by the hand to bring them out of the land of Egypt – a covenant that they broke, though I was their husband, says the Lord. But this is the covenant that I will make with the house of Israel after those days, says the Lord: I will put my law within them, and I will write it on their hearts; and I will be their God, and they shall be my people. No longer shall they teach one another, or say to each other, 'Know the Lord', for they shall all know me, from the least of them to the greatest, says the Lord; for I will forgive their iniquity, and remember their sin no more.

The following may be recited or sung to the tune 'Veni Creator'

Come Holy Spirit

Come, Holy Spirit, our souls inspire,
and lighten with eternal fire.
Implant in us your grace from above,
enter our minds and hearts with love.

O come, anointing Spirit of peace,
well-spring of life and gentleness.
Past ages called you the Paraclete,
with sevenfold gifts you make us complete.

You are the Power of God's right hand,
Promise of God to Church and land.
Life-giving words to us impart,
illumine and transform our heart.

Into our souls your love now pour,
refresh our weak frame with strength and power.
Give grace and courage to endure,
cast far away our deadly foe.

Grant us your peace through every day;
with you as Guide upon the way,
evil no more our souls shall harm.
Then shall know as we are known.

Teach us the Trinity to know,
Father, Son and Spirit, too:
the Three in One and One in Three,
now and ever, eternally.*

God's Word (2)

Galatians 5:14-26

For the whole law is summed up in a single commandment, 'You shall love your neighbour as yourself.' If, however, you bite and devour one another, take care that you are not consumed by one another.

---

*Adapted by Ray Simpson from *Veni Creator*, ascribed to Rabanus Maurus, a sixth-century Solitary in Gaul

Live by the Spirit, I say, and do not gratify the desires of the flesh. For what the flesh desires is opposed to the Spirit, and what the Spirit desires is opposed to the flesh; for these are opposed to each other, to prevent you from doing what you want. But if you are led by the Spirit, you are not subject to the law. Now the works of the flesh are obvious: fornication, impurity, licentiousness, idolatry, sorcery, enmities, strife, jealousy, anger, quarrels, dissensions, factions, envy, drunkenness, carousing, and things like these. I am warning you, as I warned you before: those who do such things will not inherit the kingdom of God.

By contrast, the fruit of the Spirit is love, joy, peace, patience, kindness, generosity, faithfulness, gentleness, and self-control. There is no law against such things. And those who belong to Christ Jesus have crucified the flesh with its passions and desires. If we live by the Spirit, let us also be guided by the Spirit. Let us not become conceited, competing against one another, envying one another.

There may be meditation or singing

Intercession

Spirit of Truth, look down upon a world
in thrall to lies and illusions.

**Work in the darkness to bring all things
into light.**

Anointing Spirit,
distribute among us your gifts:

**Wisdom, understanding and strength;
knowledge, reverence and insight.**

There may be silence, the use of spiritual gifts or singing

Great Creator of the blood-red moon
and falling stars,
Great Saviour of the miraculous birth
and rising from death,
Great Spirit of the seers and sacred words,

**Come into our minds,
come into our dreams,
come into our mouths,
until we become your presence and sign.**

Comforting Spirit,
come to all who pass through trial
and to those we love.

*Names may be mentioned
There may be singing
The following blessing may be said or sung*

**Into the life of the Three I immerse you.
May their breath be yours to live.
May their love be yours to give.**

WEDNESDAY NIGHT PRAYER

In the name of the God of wholeness,
in the name of Compassion's Son,
in the name of the healing Spirit,
tonight may we be one.

**Christ is always present when we gather
in his name.
Tonight we welcome him as healer.**

There may be singing

*Bless the Holy One, O my soul,
and all that is within me bless God's holy name.
Bless the Holy One, O my soul,
and forget not all God's benefits –
who forgives all your sins
and who heals all your diseases,
who redeems your life and crowns you with mercy,
who satisfies you with good as long as you live,
so that your youth is renewed like the eagle's.*

From Psalm 103:1-5

Let us pray for the healing
of what is fragmented in our own lives.
Father, for the ways we have marred your image in us,

Forgive.

For resentment, rush and lack of trust,

Forgive.

We open ourselves in love and faith
to your healing presence, O Christ.

There may be a pause or singing

Christ always walks the world
with those who suffer.
Let us pray for broken places of the world.

Names may be mentioned

Heal these places

**Of the lust for gain that demeans,
and of the bitterness of revenge that destroys.**

God's Word

Mark 2:1-12

When he returned to Capernaum after some days, it was reported that he was at home. So many gathered around that there was no longer room for them, not even in front of the door; and he was speaking the word to them. Then some people came, bringing to him a paralysed man, carried by four of them. And when they could not bring him to Jesus because of the crowd, they removed the roof above him; and after having dug through it, they let down the mat on which the paralytic lay. When Jesus saw their faith, he said to the paralytic, 'Son, your sins are forgiven.' Now some of the scribes were sitting there, questioning in their hearts, 'Why does this fellow speak in this way? It is blasphemy! Who can forgive sins but God alone?' At once Jesus perceived in his spirit that they were discussing these questions among themselves; and he said to them, 'Why do you raise such questions in your hearts? Which is easier, to say to the paralytic, "Your sins are forgiven", or to say, "Stand up and take your mat and walk"? But so that you may know the Son of Man has authority on earth to forgive sins' – he said to the paralytic – 'I say to you, stand up, take your mat and go to your home.' And he stood up, and immediately took the mat and went out before all of them; so that they were all amazed and glorified God, saying, 'We have never seen anything like this!'

Let us circle in healing prayer
those known to us whom we now name.

Names may be mentioned

**Spirit of the living God,
present with us now, circle these we have named.
Enter their body, mind and spirit
and heal them of all that harms.**

There may be singing

Great Spirit, who broods over the sleeping world,
as we sleep this night
**Restore the garment of our self-respect
and remake us in your beauty.**

Renew in us as we sleep
**The stillness of our being,
the soundness of our bodies,
and bring to dawn our wholeness.***

---

*A service of healing and wholeness with the laying on of hands is on
p.61 of Volume 3 of The Celtic Prayer Book: *Healing the Land*.

THURSDAY – GOD IN COMMUNITY

It was on a Thursday that Jesus prayed for unity, spoke of himself, the Father and the Spirit as a Co-unity in God, and instituted Holy Communion. So on Thursdays we pray for unity, community and sacrament at the heart of the world.

THURSDAY MORNING PRAYER

Birther of the human race
you summon the day to dawn
and call us to live in communion.

**Thrice holy God, eternal Three in One,
make your people holy, make your people one.
Stir up in us the flame that burns out pride
and power,
restore in us the trust that brings the servant
heart to flower.
Thrice holy God, come as the morning dew,
inflame in us your love
that draws all lesser loves to you.**

Thanksgiving

There may be singing

Psalm

God, be gracious to us and bless us.
May your face shine upon us.

Make known your ways on earth,
your saving health among all nations.

**May all the peoples praise you, O God.
May all the peoples praise you.**

May the nations be glad and sing for joy,
For you rule the peoples justly
and guide the nations upon earth.

**May all the peoples praise you, O God.
May all the peoples praise you.**

Then the land will yield its produce
and our God will bless us.
You will bless us,
and the ends of the earth will honour you.

Psalm 67

**Glory to the Father, to the Son
and to the Spirit,
one God who mothers us all.**

Forgiveness

We confess to you, O God,
that our lives and the world are fragmented by sin.

There may be a pause

Source of all

Have mercy on us.

Saviour of all

Have mercy on us.

Sustainer of all

Have mercy on us

The Saviour reaches out his hand
to announce a loving reconciliation.

Thanks be to God.

God's Word (1)

Isaiah 56:1-8

Thus says the Lord:
Maintain justice, and do what is right,
for soon my salvation will come,
and my deliverance be revealed.

Happy is the mortal who does this,
the one who holds it fast,
who keeps the sabbath, not profaning it,
and refrains from doing any evil.

Do not let the foreigner joined to the Lord say,
'The Lord will surely separate me from his people';
and do not let the eunuch say,
'I am just a dry tree.'
For thus says the Lord:

To the eunuchs who keep my sabbaths,
who choose the things that please me
and hold fast my covenant,
I will give, in my house and within my walls,
a monument and a name
better than sons and daughters;
I will give them an everlasting name
that shall not be cut off.

And the foreigners who join themselves to the Lord,
to minister to him, to love the name of the Lord,
and to be his servants,
all who keep the sabbath, and do not profane it,
and hold fast my covenant –
these I will bring to my holy mountain,
and make them joyful in my house of prayer;
their burnt-offerings and their sacrifices
will be accepted on my altar;
for my house shall be called a house of prayer
for all peoples.
Thus says the Lord God,
who gathers the outcasts of Israel,
I will gather others to them
besides those already gathered.

Happy the People

May our sons be like the plants that grow up strong.

Happy the people whose God is the Eternal Source.

May our daughters be like pillars that grace a palace.

Happy the people whose God is the Eternal Source.

May our stores be filled with worthy goods.

Happy the people whose God is the Eternal Source.

May creatures and crops grow into well-being.

Happy the people whose God is the Eternal Source.

May our streets be free from clamour and crime.

Happy the people whose God is the Eternal Source.

From Psalm 144

God's Word (2)

Romans 12:4-18

For as in one body we have many members, and not all the members have the same function, so we, who are many, are one body in Christ, and individually we are members one of another. We have gifts that differ according to the grace given to us: prophecy, in proportion to faith; ministry in ministering; the teacher, in teaching; the exhorter, in exhortation; the giver, in generosity; the leader, in diligence; the compassionate, in cheerfulness.

Let love be genuine; hate what is evil, hold fast to what is good; love one another with mutual affection; outdo one another in showing honour. Do not lag in zeal, be ardent in spirit, serve the Lord. Rejoice in hope, be patient in suffering, persevere in prayer. Contribute to the needs of the saints; extend hospitality to strangers.

Bless those who persecute you; bless and do not curse them.

Rejoice with those who rejoice, weep with those who weep. Live in harmony with one another; do not be haughty, but associate with the lowly; do not claim to be wiser than you are. Do not repay anyone evil for evil, but take thought for what is noble in the sight of all. If it is possible, so far as it depends on you, live peaceably with all.

There may be meditation or singing

Intercession

After any of the following responses, examples of current concerns may be offered to God

Ground of all being, all peoples come from you.
May we honour one another and seek the common good.

Reconciler of all people –
employers, employees and shareholders
are like fingers on your hands.
**May the wealth and work of the world
be available to all and for the exploitation of none.**

Unity of the world, from you all peace,
all justice flow.
**May we cherish the web of life and respect
the rule of law.**

There may be singing

Eternal God and Father,
you create us by your power
and redeem us by your love:
guide and strengthen us by your Spirit
that we may give ourselves in love and service
to one another and to you.

The following blessing may be said or sung
Into the Sacred Three I immerse you.
Into their power and peace I place you.

May their breath be ours to live.
May their love be ours to give.
Into the Sacred Three I immerse you

THURSDAY MIDDAY PRAYER

There may be singing

God of justice, God of peace,
in the heat of the day
we take refuge in you.

Glory to you, Father.
Glory to you.
Glory to you, Saviour.
Glory to you.
Glory to you, Spirit.
Glory to you.

How good it is, how pleasing,
for God's people to live together in harmony.
It is like precious ointment running down a face.
It is like dew falling on the hills.

From Psalm 133

We weave this day,
Silence of knowing,
clearness of seeing,
grace of speaking.

Pause

We weave this day,
Humility of listening,
depth of understanding,
joy of serving.

Pause

We weave this day,
Peace of being,
gift of loving,
power of meeting.

Pause

Jesus said: 'Where two or three come together
in my name I am there.'   *Matthew 18:20*

'Do for others what you want them to do for you.'

Matthew 7:12

There may be meditation
All may say, or sing, to the tune 'Bunessan'

Christ be within me,
Christ be beside me,
Christ in the stranger,
Christ in the friend,
Christ in my speaking,
Christ in my thinking,
Christ in my working,
Christ at my end.

God of community,
Spirit of energy and change,
pour on us, without reserve or distinction,
that we may have strength to plant your justice
on earth.

Your kingdom come,
your will be done,
on earth, as it is in heaven.

Your kingdom come.

Your kingdom come in the people or situations
we now name.

Your kingdom come in . . .

People or situations may be named aloud or silently

The Three who are over our head,
the Three who provide our bread,
be with us wherever we tread.

THURSDAY EVENING PRAYER

Holy, holy, holy is the eternal Flame undying,
burning here among us in sacrificial love.

Candles may be lit

Thanksgiving

We give you thanks, Kindling Light,
that you led our forebears in the Faith
through a cloud by day and a fire by night,
and that you ever lead your people on.
We give you thanks that you have led us
to this place.
Pour forth your kindness on your people,
Father, Saviour, and radiant Spirit.

There may be singing

Psalm 82

God has taken his place in the divine council;
in the midst of the gods he holds judgement;
'How long will you judge unjustly
and show partiality to the wicked?
Selah

Give justice to the weak and the orphan;
maintain the right of the lowly and the destitute.
Rescue the weak and the needy;
deliver them from the hand of the wicked.'

They have neither knowledge nor understanding,
they walk around in darkness;
all the foundations of the earth are shaken.

I say, 'You are gods,
children of the Most High, all of you;
nevertheless, you shall die like mortals,
and fall like any prince.'

Rise up, O God, judge the earth;
for all the nations belong to you!

Forgiveness

We offer to you, Lord, the troubles of this day;
we lay down our burdens at your feet.
Forgive us our sins, give us your peace,
and help us to receive your Word.

In the name of Christ.
Amen.

God's Word (1)

Isaiah 51:4-6

Listen to me, my people,
and give heed to me, my nation;
for a teaching will go out from me,
and my justice for a light to the peoples.

I will bring near my deliverance swiftly,
my salvation has gone out
and my arms will rule the peoples;
the coastlands wait for me,
and for my arm they hope.
Lift up your eyes to the heavens,
and look at the earth beneath;
for the heavens will vanish like smoke,
the earth will wear out like a garment,
and those who live on it will die like gnats;
but my salvation will be for ever,
and my deliverance will never be ended.

Triune God Who Mothers Us All

Triune God who mothers us all,
nurture the people through your Church.
Through her pastors,

Nourish us.

Through her teachers,

Establish us.

Through her prophets,

Envision us.

Through her musicians,

Inspire us.

Through her saints,

Sanctify us.

Through her givers,

Bless us.

God's Word (2)

Galatians 3:23-28

Now before faith came, we were imprisoned and guarded under the law until faith would be revealed. Therefore the law was our disciplinarian until Christ came, so that we might be justified by faith. But now that faith has come, we are no longer subject to a disciplinarian, for in Christ Jesus you are all children of God through faith. As many of you as were baptised into Christ have clothed yourselves with Christ. There is no longer Jew or Greek, there is no longer slave or free, there is no longer male and female; for all of you are one in Christ Jesus.

There may be meditation and singing

Intercession

Lord Christ,
you prayed for the unity of all who believe:
May your churches rejoice in the communion
of heaven,
and attain communion round one table on earth.
Lord Christ,
you call us to love our neighbours:
May our local communities
seek the common good.
Lord Christ,
through bread and wine you give us signs
of your Presence
transforming all creation:

May artists and those in the media
glimpse this vision,
and reflect it to the world.

One or more of the following may be said

O God, grant us unity.
Bless the oppressed,
bless the oppressor.
Draw all people home to you.
Deliver the oppressed,
pity the unnoticed,
raise the fallen,
show yourself to the needy,
heal the sick,
bring back those who have strayed,
feed the hungry,
lift up the weak,
remove the prisoners' chains.
May every people come to know that you are God,
that Jesus Christ is your Child,
that we are your people.

Clement of Rome, c.200

May petty ways drop from us like scales
until we seek the greatness of others,
we rejoice in being givers,
heaven delights in our pleasure.

**May our nation find your will as her destiny,
and God-guided representatives at home
and abroad.**

May she find peace within herself
and become a peacemaker
in the international family.

Lord Jesus Christ, Light of the world,
by your cross you have overcome
all darkness that oppresses.

**Come and shine on us in our communities
that we may grow and live together in your love
which makes us one with all humanity.**

There may be singing

**The grace of our Lord Jesus Christ,
the love of God,
and the fellowship of the Holy Spirit
be with us all evermore. Amen.**

THURSDAY NIGHT PRAYER

Three candles may be lit as the following words are said

I light a light in the name of the Father
who fosters us.
I light a light in the name of the Saviour
who embraces us.
I light a light in the name of the Spirit
who encircles us.

One is the God from whom all people come.
One earth is the bed on which we make
our home.
One is the air that all creatures breathe.

On your world, Lord,

Your love descend this night.

On your Church, Lord,

Your love descend this night.

On all who work, Lord,

Your love descend this night.

Where there is strife, Lord,

Your love descend this night.

Where there is neglect, Lord,

Your love descend this night.

On all who sleep, Lord,

Your love descend this night.

Mighty One, I give you thanks with my whole heart.
Great are your works: all who sense their wonder
    study them.
Your work overflows with majesty and honour
and your righteousness lasts for ever.
You are gracious and full of mercy.
You provide food for those who honour you.
You are faithful and just in what you do.
Reverence for you is the beginning of wisdom;
all those who practise it have good understanding.
                                      From Psalm 111

There may be singing

We thank you for your presence through the day
and for friends who have helped us on our way.
As shadows fall
and the wheels of the world grow still,
forgive us for our failures in love.

**Visit this house and drive away
all that would harm.
May holy angels preserve us in peace.**

Support us, Lord,
through life's troubled day,
until the shadows lengthen
and evening comes,
the fever of life is over
and our work is done.
Then, Lord, in your mercy,
give us a holy rest,
and peace at the last.

After a prayer of Cardinal Newman

There may be silence

Romans 12:15-17

*Rejoice with those who rejoice, weep with those who weep. Live
in harmony with one another; do not be haughty, but associate
with the lowly; do not claim to be wiser than you are. Do not
repay anyone evil for evil, but take thought for what is noble in
the sight of all.*

Circle the world, Lord,
**Keep grudges without,
keep friendship within.**
Circle the world, Lord,
**Keep wrangling without,
keep trust within.**
Circle those we bring before you now.

Names may be mentioned and there may be singing

Kindle in our hearts, O God,
the flame of that love which never ceases;
that it may burn in us this night,
till we shine for ever in your presence.

God with us lying down,
God with us rising up,
Christ with us sleeping,
Christ with us waking,
Spirit with us now,
Spirit with us evermore.

FRIDAY – THE CROSS

On a Friday, Jesus the Christ, Son of God, was put to death on a cross. In common with the universal Church, Christians in the Celtic tradition make themselves one with Christ's suffering on Fridays, and also with the suffering and broken people of the world.

Aidan's disciples ate no food until 3pm on Fridays in order to develop empathy with Christ and time for meditation.

FRIDAY MORNING PRAYER

On this day of Christ's suffering and death,
let us be one with him in his wounds.

We seek to tread in the steps of Christ
who has shown us the way, when strong, when weak.

The Servant Leader

Who has believed what we heard foretold about
the arm of God?

He grew up before God like a tender shoot;
like a root out of dry ground.

He had no beauty or majesty to attract us to him;
nothing in his appearance to make us desire him.

People despised and rejected him.
He was a man of sorrows, steeped in grief.
Like someone from whom people avert their gaze,
he was looked down upon and given no esteem.

Yet even though we thought God had afflicted him
and cast him down,
there is no doubt that he took our frailties
and carried our sorrows.

He was pierced for our sins,
he was crushed for our wrongdoing.
His punishment brought peace to us;
we are healed by his wounds.

Like sheep we have all gone astray,
we have each followed our own way
and God has pinned our failings on to him.

After his soul-suffering he will see the light of joy.
This righteous servant will put right many people.

He will be ranked with the greatest
because he poured out his life and his prayers for us.

Isaiah 53:1-6; 11-12

Glory to the Maker,
glory to the Son,
glory to the Spirit,
ever Three and ever One.

Forgiveness

Jesus, you were driven to the sands
by the searching Spirit.
Strip from us what is not of you.

Confession is made in silence, or as follows

Forgive us for our selfish deeds,
our empty speech
and the words with which we have wounded.

Pause

**Forgive us for our false desires,
our vengeful attitudes
and for what we have left untended.**

There may be a pause

Holy Jesus, hanged on a tree, victorious over death,
forgive us for these sins,
free us from these evils,
and power us into new ways.

There may be singing

God's Word (1)

Genesis 22:1-14

After these things God tested Abraham. He said to him, 'Abraham!' And he said, 'Here I am.' He said, 'Take your son, your only son Isaac, whom you love, and go to the land of Moriah, and offer him there as a burnt-offering on one of the mountains that I shall show you.' So Abraham rose early in the morning, saddled his donkey, and took two of his young men with him, and his son Isaac; he cut the wood for the burnt-offering, and set out and went to the place in the distance that God had shown him. On the third day Abraham looked up and saw the place far away. Then Abraham said to his young men, 'Stay here with the donkey; the boy and I will go over there; we will worship, and then we will come back to you.' Abraham took the wood of the burnt-offering and laid it on his son Isaac, and he himself carried the fire and the knife. So the two of them walked on together. Isaac said to his father Abraham, 'Father!' And he said, 'Here I am, my son.' He said, 'The fire and the wood are here, but where is the lamb for a burnt-offering?' Abraham said, 'God himself will provide the lamb for a burnt-offering, my son.' So the two of them walked on together.

When they came to the place that God had shown him, Abraham built an altar there and laid the wood in order. He bound his son Isaac, and laid him on the altar, on top of the wood. Then Abraham reached out his hand and took the knife to kill his son. But the angel of the Lord called to him from heaven, and said, 'Abraham, Abraham!' And he said, 'Here I am.' He said, 'Do not lay your hand on the boy or do anything to him; for now I know that you fear God, since you have not withheld your son, your only son, from me.' And Abraham looked up and saw a ram, caught in a thicket by its horns. Abraham went and took the ram and offered it up as a burnt-offering instead of his son. So Abraham called that place 'The Lord will provide'; as it is said to this day, 'On the mount of the Lord it shall be provided.'

Jesus, Saviour of the World

Jesus, Saviour of the world,
come to us in your mercy.
We look to you to save and help us.

By your cross and life laid down,
you set your people free.
We look to you to save and help us.

When your disciples were about to perish,
you reached down and saved them.
We look to you to come to our help.

In the greatness of your mercy,
free us from our chains.
Forgive the sins of all your people.

Come now, and dwell with us, Lord Christ Jesus.
Hear our prayer and be with us always.

And when you come in your glory,
**Make us to be one with you
and to share the life of your kingdom.**

God's Word (2)

John 19:16-30

Then he handed him over to them to be crucified.

So they took Jesus; and carrying the cross by himself, he went out to what is called The Place of the Skull, which in Hebrew is called Golgotha. There they crucified him, and with

111

him two others, one on either side, with Jesus between them. Pilate also had an inscription written and put on the cross. It read, 'Jesus of Nazareth, the King of the Jews.' Many of the Jews read this inscription, because the place where Jesus was crucified was near the city; and it was written in Hebrew, in Latin, and in Greek. Then the chief priests of the Jews said to Pilate, 'Do not write, "The King of the Jews", but "This man said, I am King of the Jews."' Pilate answered, 'What I have written I have written.' When the soldiers had crucified Jesus, they took his clothes and divided them into four parts, one for each soldier. They also took his tunic; now the tunic was seamless, woven in one piece from the top. So they said to one another, 'Let us not tear it, but cast lots for it to see who will get it.' This was to fulfil what the scripture says,

'They divided my clothes among themselves,
and for my clothing they cast lots.'

And that is what the soldiers did.

Meanwhile, standing near the cross of Jesus were his mother, and his mother's sister, Mary the wife of Clopas, and Mary Magdalene. When Jesus saw his mother and the disciple whom he loved standing beside her, he said to his mother, 'Woman, here is your son.' Then he said to the disciple, 'Here is your mother.' And from that hour the disciple took her into his own home.

After this, when Jesus knew that all was now finished, he said (in order to fulfil the scripture), 'I am thirsty.' A jar full of sour wine was standing there. So they put a sponge full of the wine on a branch of hyssop and held it to his mouth. When Jesus had received the wine, he said, 'It is finished.' Then he bowed his head and gave up his spirit.

There may be silence

Intercession

Jesus, broken on the cross,
we bring to you those suffering
from broken dreams,
broken relationships
and broken promises.

There may be silence or any may mention names

Jesus,
Have mercy on them.

Jesus, who lost everything,
we bring to you those who have suffered
loss of work, mobility and well-being.

There may be silence or names may be mentioned

Jesus,
Have mercy on them.

Jesus, Defenceless victim,
we bring to you those who are victims
of violence, abuse and false accusation.

There may be silence or names may be mentioned

Jesus,
Have mercy on them.

113

Jesus, alone and destitute,
we bring to you those who are lonely,
homeless and hungry.

There may be silence or names may be mentioned

Jesus,
Have mercy on them.

Saviour, you died that we
may be brought back to you.
Save and raise up those who
have none but you to turn to.

Jesus,
Have mercy on them.

The Lord's Prayer may be said.
There may be singing

May the Christ who walks with wounded feet,
walk with us on the road.
May the Christ who serves with wounded hands
stretch out our hands to serve.
May the Christ who loves with wounded heart
open our hearts to love.

FRIDAY MIDDAY PRAYER

Jesus, Master Carpenter of Nazareth,
who, through wood and nails,
won our full salvation,
wield well your tools in this your workshop
that we who come to you rough hewn
may here be fashioned into a truer beauty
by your hand.

Psalm: 31:1-5

In you, O Lord, I seek refuge;
do not let me ever be put to shame;
in your righteousness deliver me.
Incline your ear to me;
rescue me speedily.
Be a rock of refuge for me,
a strong fortress to save me.

You are indeed my rock and my fortress;
for your name's sake lead me and guide me,
take me out of the net that is hidden for me,
for you are my refuge.
Into your hand I commit my spirit;
you have redeemed me, O Lord,
faithful God.

There may be silence or singing

We draw aside in the midst of the day.
We weep for the hungry and poor;
the children mistreated, those broken by force;
and the maimed who can't finish their course.

**We plead for your justice to fill all the lands
as the waters cover the sands.**

We pray against cruelty, hatred and pain;
against pride and greed for gain.
We pray for the homeless and victims of war;
the strangers to love at the door.

**We plead for your justice to fill all the lands
as the waters cover the sands.**

Andrew Dick

Lord Jesus,
at this hour you hung on the cross,
stretching out your arms in love to all.
May the peoples of the world be drawn to your
uplifted love,
especially those with whom we shall work this day.

**Give us the will to share our bread
with the hungry,
to give shelter to those who feel rejected,
and to reach out to those in need.**

We pray for those whose tasks are backbreaking,
whose bodies are mutilated
or whose spirits are crushed.

During a silence, think of the hungry, the poor and the oppressed, and Jesus on the cross in solidarity with them.

There may be free prayer followed by these words of Jesus

Happy you who hunger for justice –
You will be filled.
Happy you who show mercy –
You will receive mercy.
Happy you who weep for the world –
You will laugh.

There may be singing

Lord Jesus,
in the midst of mockery and madness,
you found peace to remain in your Father's will.

In the midst of a fretful day
give us peace to remain in our Father's will.

Our Father in heaven,
honoured be your name.
Your kingdom come,
your will be done
on earth, as in heaven.
Give us this day our daily supplies,
and forgive us our sins
as we forgive those who sin against us.
Lead us not into time of trial,
but deliver us from evil.

**For yours is the kingdom,
the power and the glory,
for ever and ever.
Amen.**

FRIDAY EVENING PRAYER

Sacrificial Love lingers still among us,
Calling us to wait and to watch.

Eternal Light,
Shine into our hearts.
Eternal Goodness,
Deliver us from evil.
Eternal Power,
Strengthen us.
Eternal Wisdom,
Scatter the darkness of our ignorance.
Eternal Pity,
Have mercy on us.
With our whole being we shall seek your face,
Until we are brought to your holy Presence.

After Alcuin

There may be a meditative chant or singing

Psalm

*O Lord, you have searched me and known me.
You know when I sit down and when I rise up;*

you discern my thoughts from far away.
You search out my path and my lying down,
and are acquainted with all my ways.
Even before a word is on my tongue,
O Lord, you know it completely.
You hem me in, behind and before,
and lay your hand upon me.
Such knowledge is too wonderful for me;
it is so high that I cannot attain it.

Where can I go from your spirit?
Or where can I flee from your presence?
If I ascend to heaven, you are there;
if I make my bed in Sheol, you are there.
If I take the wings of the morning
and settle at the farthest limits of the sea,
even there your hand shall lead me,
and your right hand shall hold me fast.
If I say, 'Surely the darkness shall cover me,
and the light around me become night',
even the darkness is not dark to you;
the night is as bright as the day,
for darkness is as light to you.

For it was you who formed my inward parts;
you knit me together in my mother's womb . . .
Search me, O God, and know my heart;
test me and know my thoughts.
See if there is any wicked way in me,
and lead me in the way everlasting.

There may be silence

Psalm 139:1-13, 23-24

God's Word (1)
Lamentations 3:25-40

The Lord is good to those who wait for him,
to the soul that seeks him.
It is good that one should wait quietly
for the salvation of the Lord.
It is good for one to bear the yoke in youth,
to sit alone in silence
when the Lord has imposed it,
to put one's mouth to the dust
(there may yet be hope),
to give one's cheek to the smiter,
and be filled with insults.
For the Lord will not
reject for ever.
Although he causes grief, he will have compassion
according to the abundance of his steadfast love;
for he does not willingly afflict
or grieve anyone.

When all the prisoners of the land
are crushed under foot,
when human rights are perverted
in the presence of the Most High,
when one's case is subverted
– does the Lord not see it?

Who can command and have it done,
if the Lord has not ordained it?
Is it not from the mouth of the Most High
that good and bad come?

Why should any who draw breath complain
about the punishment of their sins?

Let us test and examine our ways,
and return to the Lord.

Forgiveness

Lord, you were tested by the evil one.

Break in us the hold of power and pride.

You knew deep tears and weaknesses.

Help us to be vulnerable for you.

You followed to the end the Way of the Cross.

Help us to be faithful to you to the end of our days.

A Kyrie may be sung

God's Word (2)

John 10:11-18

'I am the good shepherd. The good shepherd lays down his life
for the sheep.
    The hired hand, who is not the shepherd and does not own
the sheep, sees the wolf coming and leaves the sheep and runs
away – and the wolf snatches them and scatters them. The hired
hand runs away because a hired hand does not care for the sheep.
I am the good shepherd. I know my own and my own know me,

just as the Father knows me and I know the Father. And I lay down my life for the sheep. I have other sheep that do not belong to this fold. I must bring them also, and they will listen to my voice. So there will be one flock, one shepherd. For this reason the Father loves me, because I lay down my life in order to take it up again.

No one takes it from me, but I lay it down of my own accord. I have power to lay it down, and I have power to take it up again. I have received this command from my Father.'

There may be meditation or singing

Intercession

Lord, teach us to understand that your Son died
to save us, not from suffering, but from ourselves;
not from injustice, but from being unjust.
He died that we might live as he did, who died to
   himself.

George MacDonald

**In union with witnesses and martyrs of Christ,
in communion with all who have died
in the faith of Christ,
we commit ourselves to our living God.**

As we struggle to be faithful to you and to
establish justice,
we bring to you those who are in chains.

There may be a pause or free prayer

We bring to you people who are persecuted
or oppressed, the homeless, the hungry
and those in grinding poverty.

There may be a pause or free prayer

We bring to you those who are in pain
behind closed doors.

**Lord Jesus, you were released from the pain
of the cross.
In you may the suffering find release.**

We bring to you those who are locked into hatred

**Calm their hatred.
Fill their hearts and ours with generous love.**

There may be singing

We go in the sign of the cross of Christ
   (*make sign*):
**the cross before us to keep us true,
the cross behind us to shield us from ill,
the cross above us to lead us through.**

FRIDAY NIGHT PRAYER

There may be singing

Shadows darken this day:
The day Christ was laid in a grave.
The darkness shall not engulf us,
For with you the darkness is light.

Lord, by your cross and precious death,
**Save us from the powers of evil,
save us from another's harm,
save us from our selfish failings.
Come this night and give us calm.**

Psalm 90:1-12
*Lord, you have been our dwelling-place
in all generations.
Before the mountains were brought forth,
or ever you had formed the earth and the world,
from everlasting to everlasting you are God.*

*You turn us back to dust,
and say, 'Turn back, you mortals.'
For a thousand years in your sight
are like yesterday when it is past,
or like a watch in the night.*

*You sweep them away: they are like a dream,
like grass that is renewed in the morning;
in the morning it flourishes and is renewed;
in the evening it fades and withers.*

*For we are consumed by your anger;
by your wrath we are overwhelmed.
You have set our iniquities before you,
our secret sins in the light of your countenance.*

*For all our days pass away under your wrath;
our years come to an end like a sigh.*

The days of our life are seventy years,
or perhaps eighty, if we are strong;
even then their span is only toil and trouble;
they are soon gone, and we fly away.
Who considers the power of your anger?
Your wrath is as great as the fear that is due you.
So teach us to count our days
that we may gain a wise heart.

Give us sorrow for our sins against human dignity and
   hospitality,
Give us sorrow for the sins of this day,

That when our bodies become but ashes
we may live with you for ever.

Let us reflect on the things that
distance us from Christ.

There may be a silent examination of conscience

Forgive us our sins.
Lord, forgive.

Words such as 'Lord, have mercy' or 'Kyrie eleison'
may be sung

As he was dying, Jesus said:
My God, my God, why have you forsaken me?
Christ forsaken,
Have mercy on all who are forsaken.

Christ afraid,

Have mercy on all who are afraid.

Christ betrayed,

Have mercy on all who are betrayed.

Christ unnoticed,

Have mercy on all who are unnoticed.

*People may mention names of those who need prayers, in
silence or aloud*
Great God who mothers us all,
gather the sufferings of all
into the communion of the crucified Christ.
**Shield and deliver them
and look on them with your merciful gaze.**

There may be singing

I will pour out a spirit of compassion and
prayer on the inhabitants,
so that when they look on the one
whom they have pierced,
they shall mourn for him
as one mourns for an only child.

Zechariah 12:10

**For love is as strong as death,
passion fierce as the grave . . .
Many waters cannot quench love.**

Song of Songs 8:6-7

Jesus said: Father, into your hands
I commit my life.

Father, into your hands we commit our lives.

Father, at the foot of your Son's cross,
help us to see and know your love for us.

Father, into your hands we commit our lives.

At last, all-powerful Master,
**you give leave to your servant
to go in peace according to your promise.
For my eyes have seen your salvation,
which you have prepared for all nations –
a light to illumine the world
and give glory to your people.**

O Christ,
who at this evening hour rested in the tomb
and made it become a bed of hope,
visit this house tonight,
that we may pass through the death of sleep
and rise from our beds in hope of life eternal.

**Then, Lord, give us a peaceful night
and a good ending to life.**

I make the sign of the cross of Christ (*make sign*):

**My Christ,
my Shield,
my Saviour;
each day, each night,
in light, in dark;
my treasure,
my dear One,
my eternal home.**

SATURDAY – GOD'S RULE ON EARTH AND IN HEAVEN

For many people Saturday is a time for leisure, shopping or converse with the world. Morning and Midday Prayer reflect these pursuits.

The week is drawing to a close, and we prepare to move into a higher plane.

Evening and Night Prayer introduce the theme of converse with the saints.

SATURDAY MORNING PRAYER

Life-giving God, the world lies open before you,

And you summon the day to dawn.

Open our being

And we shall show life.

Open our hearts

And we shall show love.

Open our mouths

And we shall show praise.

There may be singing

Psalm

Creator God, how great you are!
You clothe yourself in light,
you stretch out the skies like a tent.

**Winds are your messengers,
flames are your servants.**

You water the earth,
you bring food for us from the earth.

**How abundant are your works, O God,
in wisdom have you made them all –
the creatures, teeming the earth.**

There is the sea, vast and wide,
innumerable things, small and great,
    live within it.

**All these look to you for their food in due season.
When you send forth your Spirit they are created,
and you renew the face of the earth.**

May your glory last for ever.
May you always have joy in what you have created.

May our thoughts always give you pleasure,
may we always rejoice in you.

From Psalm 104

All That Moves, Bless Your God

All that moves on the earth,
Bless your God.
All that swims in the water,
Bless your God.
All that flies in the air,
Give glory to God who nurtures us all.

Parents and children,
Bless your God.
Friends and lovers,
Bless your God.
Musicians and sportsfolk,
Give glory to God who nurtures us all.

Parks and play areas,
Bless your God.
Streets and shops,
Bless your God.
Homes and gardens,
Give glory to God who nurtures us all.

God's Word (1)

Isaiah 66:12-14

For thus says the Lord:
I will extol prosperity to her like a river,
and the wealth of the nations like an overflowing stream;
and you shall nurse and be carried on her arm,
and dandled on her knees.
As a mother comforts her child,
so I will comfort you;
you shall be comforted in Jerusalem.
You shall see, and your heart shall rejoice;
your bodies shall flourish like the grass;
and it shall be known that the hand of the Lord is with his
*   servants,*
and his indignation is against his enemies.

We Believe

We believe, O God of all gods,
that you are the eternal God of life.

We believe, O God of all peoples,
that you are the eternal God of love.

We believe that you create earth
and seas and skies.

We believe that you create us in your image,
and give us eternal worth.
We honour you with our whole being
and consecrate this day to you.

God's Word (2)

Matthew 7:7-13

Ask, and it will be given to you; search, and you will find; knock, and the door will be opened for you. For everyone who asks receives, and everyone who searches finds, and for everyone who knocks, the door will be opened. Is there anyone among you who, if your child asks for bread, will give a stone? Or if the child asks for a fish, will give a snake? If you, then, who are evil, know how to give good gifts to your children, how much more will your Father in heaven give good things to those who ask him!

In everything do to others as you would have them do to you; for this is the law and the prophets.

Enter through the narrow gate; for the gate is wide and the road is easy that leads to destruction, and there are many who take it.

There may be meditation and singing

Intercession

Make whole the leisure and activity of this day;
restrain its hostile impulses,
fill its moments.

There may be silent reflection

Our Father in heaven,
hallowed be your name.
Your kingdom come,
your will be done,
on earth, as in heaven.

In our pleasures,
Your kingdom come.
In our leaders,
Your kingdom come.
In our gatherings,
Your kingdom come.
On the roads,
Your kingdom come.
On the networks,
Your kingdom come.
In each thing we do this day,
In . . . (*examples may be mentioned*)
Your kingdom come.

Give us this day our daily supplies,
and forgive us our sins
as we forgive those who sin against us.
Lead us not into temptation,
but deliver us from evil.
**For the kingdom, the power and the glory
are yours,
now and for ever. Amen.**

There may be singing

May we do this day on earth
As the saints do in heaven.

May we live this day in your light,
And walk in the hope of your kingdom.

SATURDAY MIDDAY PRAYER

There may be silence

O Being of life!
O Being of peace!
O Being of time!
Be with us in the middle of the day.

Pause
O Being of truth,
O Being of sight,
O Being of wisdom,
Be with us in the middle of the day.

There may be singing

Psalm 119:9-16

How can young people keep their way pure?
By guarding it according to your word.
With my whole heart I seek you;
do not let me stray from your commandments.
I treasure your word in my heart,
so that I may not sin against you.
Blessed are you, O Lord;
teach me your statutes.

With my lips I declare
all the ordinances of your mouth.
I delight in the way of your decrees
as much as in all riches.
I will meditate on your precepts,
and fix my eyes on your ways.
I will delight in your statutes;
I will not forget your word.

Christ who stilled the storm,
Still the turmoil within.
Christ who overcame harm,
Overcome the evil without.

Happy you who are poor in heart;
yours is the kingdom of God.
Happy you who are clear in heart;
you will see God.

Matthew 5:3,8

There may be silence and singing

Spirit, kindle in my heart
a flame of love to my foe,
to my friend, to all.

In God is my strength;
God alone is sufficient.

Guardian,
be over the restless people
a covering of truth and peace.

There may be silence or free prayer

May the saints and the Saviour watch over us
and keep us true in all we do.

**May we live the rest of this day
in the joy of the Saviour's will.**

SATURDAY EVENING PRAYER

Let us go for a while to the courts of heaven and join with
the saints in praise.

Thanksgiving

Sing to God's glory all the earth
and offer joyful praise.

**Say to God, 'Your deeds are awesome.
Before your power even your foes fall back.'**

The whole earth worships you, O God,
and sings to you her praise.

**Look back on God's almighty deeds
among mortal human beings.**

The exiles crossed the sea dry-shod,
for God turned the ocean back.

**Then we joyed in the Mighty One,
who reigns in power for ever.**

God watches nations in their pride,
and forges us through trials.

**You journey with us through the fires,
and make us more complete.**

I offer you my all, O God,
for your love for me never fails.

From Psalm 66

**Glory to our Maker.
Glory to Christ.
Glory to the Spirit.
One God, who mothers us all.**

There may be singing

God's Word (1)

Ecclesiasticus 44:1-15

*Let us now sing the praises of famous men,
our ancestors in their generations.
The Lord apportioned to them great glory,
his majesty from the beginning.
There were those who ruled in their kingdoms,
and made a name for themselves by their valour;
those who gave counsel because they were intelligent;
those who spoke in prophetic oracles;
those who led the people by their counsels
and by their knowledge of the people's lore;
they were wise in their words of instruction;
those who composed musical tunes,*

or put verses in writing;
rich men endowed with resources,
living peacefully in their homes –
all these were honoured in their generations,
and were the pride of their times.
Some of them have left behind a name,
so that others declare their praise.
But of others there is no memory;
they have perished as though they had never existed;
they have become as though they had never been born,
they and their children after them.
But these also were godly men,
whose righteous deeds have not been forgotten;
their wealth will remain with their descendants,
and their inheritance with their children's children.
Their descendants stand by the convenants;
their children also, for their sake.
Their offspring will continue for ever,
and their glory will never be blotted out.
Their bodies are buried in peace,
but their name lives on generation
after generation.
The assembly declares their wisdom,
and the congregation proclaims their praise.

We Still Could Not Thank You Enough

If our mouths were full of song as the sea,
our tongues with joyful sounds
like the roar of its waves,
our lips with praise like the outspread sky,

**We still could not thank you enough, Yahweh,
for the good you have done to us
and our forebears.**

If our eyes were shining like the sun and the moon,
our hands stretched out like eagles' wings
in the air,
our feet as swift as the wild deer,

**We still could not thank you enough, Yahweh,
for the good you have done to us and our forebears.**

You rescued us from the tyrant.
You freed us from slavery.

**In times of famine you fed us.
In times of plenty you built us up.**

From violence you delivered us.
From plagues you saved us.

**Therefore to you who breathed life into us
we shall give praise with all our breath,
honour with all our memory,
worship with all our being.**

God's Word (2)

Hebrews 12:22-23
*But you have come to Mount Zion and to the city of the living
God, the heavenly Jerusalem, and to innumerable angels in
festal gathering, and to the assembly of the firstborn, who are
enrolled in heaven, and to God, the judge of all, and to the spirits
of the righteous made perfect.*

There may be meditation or singing

Intercession

God of the call, as we give thanks for the saints,
we pray for those who feel thwarted in their vocation.

May they do on earth as the saints do in heaven.

God from whom all truth and justice flow,
we pray for the rule of law to prevail;

May we do on earth as the saints do in heaven.

God of resurrection,
in their worship, may our churches
bring honour to you,
joy to the people,
and healing to the land.

May they do on earth as the saints do in heaven.

There may be free prayer and singing

Let us bless the Lord.

**For yours, Lord, is the glory,
the power and the majesty,
for ever and ever.
Amen.**

SATURDAY NIGHT PRAYER

On occasions when Saturday Night Prayer is extended, the reading for Sunday's main worship may be read and pondered. Or there may be the slow, thoughtful repetition of the Jesus Prayer (e.g. each person repeats it fifty times): Lord Jesus Christ, Son of God, have mercy.

Eternal Creator of the weeks and years,
as this week draws to a close, draw close to us,

And we will draw close to you.

Eternal Creator of the days and nights,
as darkness deepens, draw near to us,

And we will draw near to you.

**Most merciful God,
we confess to you,
before the company of heaven and one another,
that we have sinned in thought, word and deed,
and in what we have failed to do.
Forgive us our sins,
heal us by your Spirit,
and raise us to new life in Jesus Christ.**

Psalm 119:52-62

*When I think of your ordinances from of old,
I take comfort, O Lord.
Hot indignation seizes me because of the wicked,
those who forsake your law.
Your statutes have been my songs
wherever I make my home.
I remember your name in the night, O Lord,
and keep your law.
This blessing has fallen to me,
for I have kept your precepts.*

The Lord is my portion;
I promise to keep your words.
I implore your favour with all my heart;
be gracious to me according to your promise.
When I think of your ways,
I turn my feet to your decrees;
I hurry and do not delay
to keep your commandments.
Though the cords of the wicked ensnare me,
I do not forget your law.
At midnight I rise to praise you,
because of your righteous ordinances.

The following or another hymn may be sung or said

Before the ending of the day,
Creator of the world, we pray
that you, with steadfast love, would keep
your watch around us while we sleep.

From evil dreams defend our sight;
from fears and terror of the night.
Tread under foot our deadly foe
that we no sinful thought may know.

O Father, this we ask be done
through Jesus Christ, your only Son,
and Holy Spirit, by whose breath
our souls are raised to life from death.
Amen.

Hebrews 3:12-4:1

Take care, brothers and sisters, that none of you may have an evil, unbelieving heart that turns away from the living God.

But exhort one another every day, as long as it is called 'today', so that none of you may be hardened by the deceitfulness of sin. For we have become partners of Christ, if only we hold our first confidence firm to the end. As it is said,

> *'Today, if you hear his voice,*
> *do not harden your hearts as in*
> *the rebellion.'*

Now who were they who heard and yet were rebellious? Was it not all those who left Egypt under the leadership of Moses?

But with whom was he angry for forty years? Was it not those who sinned, whose bodies fell in the wilderness? And to whom did he swear that they would not enter his rest, if not to those who were disobedient? So we see that they were unable to enter because of unbelief.

Therefore, while the promise of entering his rest is still open, let us take care that none of you should seem to have failed to reach it.

In our tiredness be our Rest.
In our stumbling be our Shield.

Into our place of darkness,
into our place of strife,
into our fears and worries,
Come with eternal life.

Let us bring before God the concerns of this day.

These may be mentioned aloud or in silence
There may be singing

Jesus,
master of apostles,
teacher of evangelists,
strength of martyrs,
friend of the poor,
crown of saints,
lead us through the night into a day of renewal.

May we rest secure in your love
And rise up to serve you with joy.
Come with the breaking of the day
And meet us in the breaking of bread.

SIMPLE, EVERYDAY PRAYER PATTERNS FROM THE COMMUNITY OF AIDAN AND HILDA FOR MEMORISING

MORNING PRAYER

Shine on us, Lord, like the sun that lights up day;
chase away the dark and all shadow of sin.
May we wake eager to hear your Word;
as day follows night may we be bathed in your glory.

A Psalm

Read from any psalm or the following from Psalm 63:

O God, I long for you from early morning;
my whole being desires you.
Like a dry, worn-out and waterless land
my soul is thirsty for you.
Let me see you in the place of prayer;
let me see how glorious you are.
Your constant love is better than life itself,
and so I will praise you.
I will give thanks as long as I live.
I will raise my hands to you in prayer.
My soul will feast and be satisfied,
and I will sing glad songs of praise to you.

There may be singing

Illumine our hearts, O Lord;
implant in us a desire for your truth.
May all that is false within us flee.

Bible Reading(s)

*This may be followed by silence, singing,
or the Daily Meditation from* Celtic Daily Light.

Lord,
we offer you all we are, all we have,
all we do,
and all whom we shall meet this day,
that you will be given the glory.

**We offer you our homes and work,
our schools and leisure,
and everyone in our community today;
may all be done as unto you.**

We offer you the broken and hungry.
    (*names may be mentioned*)
May the wealth and work of the world
be available to all
and for the exploitation of none.
May your presence be known to all.

**Circle us, Lord,
keep strife without, keep peace within.
Keep fear without, keep hope within.
Circle us, Lord,
Keep pride without, keep trust within.
Keep evil out, keep good within.**

May we walk in the hope of your kingdom.
Fill us with your light and love.
Be with us all through this day,
Father, Son, and Holy Spirit.

MIDDAY PRAYER

We come into the presence of the creating Father.
We come into the presence of the workaday Son.
We come into the presence of the renewing Spirit.
We come into the presence of the Three in One.

Unless the Lord builds the house,
the work of the builders is useless.
Unless the Lord builds the city,
the security guards keep watch in vain.
It is useless to get up early and go to bed late;
for the Lord provides for those he loves.

Psalm 127:1,2

As the press of work pauses at noon
may God's rest be upon us.
As the sun rides high at noon,
may the Sun of Righteousness shine upon us.
As the rain refreshes the stained, stale streets
may the Spirit bring rain upon our dry ground.

There may be silence or sharing

A Bible Verse

*Read and meditate on this verse from Ephesians 6:6-7
or another verse from the Bible:*

Whatever the work you do, do it to the Lord,
with a sense of respect and responsibility
to those you work for.

The Lord's Prayer may be said

**Lead me from death to life,
from falsehood to truth.
Lead me from despair to hope,
from fear to trust.
Lead me from hate to love,
from war to peace.
Deep peace of the Son of peace
fill our hearts, our workplace, our world.**

Bless us now, Lord, in the middle of the day.
Be with us and all who are dear to us.
Keep us in the beautiful attitudes,
joyful, simple and gentle.

**May the Three of limitless love
be in the eye of each one we shall meet,
and pour upon us more and more generously
hour by hour.**

EVENING PRAYER

Spirit of the Risen Christ,
as lamps light up the evening,
shine into our hearts
and kindle in us the fire of your love.

Candles may be lit. All say or sing:

The light of Christ has come into the world!

We give you thanks that you led our forebears
in the Faith through a cloud by day and a fire by night;
we give you thanks, kindly Light, that the torch of faith
was brought to this land, and that you ever lead your
    people on.
Light up our dark hearts by the light of your Christ;
may his Word illumine our way,
for you pour forth loving-kindness upon your whole
    creation,
Father, Son and radiant Spirit.

May the Light of lights come to my dark heart;
may the Spirit's wisdom come to me from my Saviour.
May the peace of the Spirit be mine this night,
the peace of the Son be mine this night,
the peace of the Father be mine this night,
the peace of all peace be mine this night,
each morning and evening of my life.

A Psalm

We offer to you, Lord, the troubles of this day;
we lay down our burdens at your feet.

Forgive us our sins, give us your peace,
and help us to receive your Word.

A Bible Reading
You Are My Island

Lord, you are my island;

In your bosom I nest.

You are the calm of the sea;

In that peace I rest.

You are the waves on the shore's
glistening stones;

Their sound is my hymn.

You are the song of the birds;

Their tune I sing.

You are the sea breaking on rock;

I praise you with the swell.

You are the ocean that laps my being;

In you I dwell.

Thanksgiving

We give you thanks that you are always present,
in all things, each day and each night.
We give you thanks for your gifts of creation,
life and friendship.
We give you thanks for the blessings of this day (. . .)

There may be singing

Intercession

Into your hands, O Lord,
we place our families, our neighbours,
our brothers and sisters in Christ,
and all whom we have met today (. . .)
Enfold them in your will.

Into your hands, O Lord,
we place all who are victims of prejudice,
oppression or neglect;
the unwanted, the frail (. . .)
**May everyone be cherished
from conception to the grave.**

Into your hands, O Lord,
we place all who are restless,
sick, or prey to the powers of evil (. . .)
watch over them and watch over us this night.

Into your hands, O Lord,
we place these members of our Community (. . .) and
    others on our hearts (. . .)

**The grace of our Lord Jesus Christ,
the love of God,
and the fellowship of the Holy Spirit
be with us all. Amen.**

NIGHT PRAYER

In the name of the restful Father,
in the name of the calming Son,
in the name of the peaceful Spirit.
May we and God be one.

I place my soul and body
under your guarding this night, O God,
O Father of help to frail pilgrims,
Protector of heaven and earth.

**I place my soul and body
under your guiding this night, O Christ.
O Son of the tears and the woundings,
may your cross this night be my shield.**

I place my soul and body
under your glowing this night, O Spirit,
O gentle Companion, and soul Friend,
my heart's eternal Warmth.

Say or sing Psalm 134 or another psalm

**Come bless the Lord, all you servants of the Lord,
who stand by night in the house of the Lord;
lift up your hands in the holy place,
come bless the Lord, come bless the Lord.**

May that part of me that did not grow at morning,
grow at nightfall (. . .)

There may be a brief pause

You are our Saviour and Lord.
In our stumbling be our shield.
In our tiredness be our Rest.
In our darkness be our Light.

O Christ, Son of the living God,
may your holy angels guard our sleep.
May they watch over us as we rest
and hover around our beds.
Let them reveal to us in our dreams
visions of your glorious truth.
May no fears or worries delay
our willing, prompt repose.

Read these or other words of Christ:

Come to me, all you who are weary and burdened,
and I will give you rest.
Take my yoke upon you and learn from me,
for I am gentle and humble of heart,
and you will find rest for your souls.

Matthew 11: 28-29

*This may be followed by silence during which
other words from God may be spoken spontaneously*

Our dear ones bless, O God,
and keep in every place where they are (. . .)
**May the great and strong heavenly army
encircle us all with their outstretched arms
to protect us from the hostile powers,
to put balm into our dreams.
To give us contented, sweet repose.**

I lie down this night with God,
and God will lie down with me.
I lie down this night with Christ,
and Christ will lie down with me.
I lie down this night with the Spirit,
and the Spirit will lie down with me.
God and Christ and the Spirit,
lying down with me.

I make the sign of the cross of Christ.
   (*make sign of the cross*)
My Christ, my Shield, my Encircler,
each day, each night, in light, in dark,
My Treasure, my dear One.

The almighty and merciful Three circle us,
that awake we may watch with Christ,
and asleep we may rest in peace.

SOURCES

These sources have been consulted or drawn from:

A Celtic Book of Days, Sarah Costley and Charles Knightly (Thames and Hudson, 1998)

A Celtic Liturgy, Pat Robson (HarperCollins, 2000)

A Contemporary Celtic Prayer Book (Acta Publications, Chicago, Illinois, US)

A Manual of Eastern Orthodox Prayers (SPCK, 1983)

An Anglo-Saxon Passion, David Scott (SPCK, 1999)

A Wee Worship Book: Fourth Incarnation (Wild Goose Publications, 1999)

A World of Blessing: Benedictions from every Continent and Many Cultures, Geoffrey Duncan (Canterbury Press)

Called To Be Saints!: Readings for Holy Days, Raymond Foster (Church in Wales Publications, 1987)

Celebrating Common Prayer: A Version of the Daily Office SSF (Mowbray, 1992)

Celtic Benediction: Morning and Night Prayer, J. Philip Newell (Canterbury Press, 2000)

Celtic Daily Light, comp. Ray Simpson (Kevin Mayhew, 2003)

Celtic Daily Prayer from the Northumbria Community (HarperCollins, 2000)

Celtic Devotional, Caitlin Matthews (Godsfield Press, 1996)

Celtic Spirituality, Oliver Davies, trans (Paulist Press New York, 1999)

Celtic Wisdom: Seasonal Rituals and Festivals, Vivianne Crowley (Sterling, New York)

Celtic Worship Through the Year, Ray Simpson (Hodder & Stoughton, 1997)

Enriching the Christian Year, compiled by Michael Perham (SPCK / Alcuin Club, 1993)

Forms of Prayer for Jewish Worship (The Reform Synagogues of Great Britain, 1977)

Human Rites, compiled by Hannah Ward and Jennifer Wild (Mowbray, 1995)

Irish Litanies, Charles Plummer (ed. and trans.) (The Boydell Press, 1962)

Orthodox Feasts of Christ and Mary: Liturgical Texts with Commentary, Hugh Wybrew (SPCK, 1997)

Orthodox Lent, Holy Week and Easter: Liturgical Texts and Commentary, Hugh Wybrew (SPCK, 1995)

Praise in All Our Days: Common Prayer at Taizé (Mowbray, 1981)

Praying with the Celtic Saints, Mary C. Earle and Sylvia Maddox (St Mary's Press, Christian Brothers Publications, Minnesota)

The Antiphonary of Bangor and the Early Irish Monastic Liturgy, Michael Curran (Irish Academic Press, 1984)

The Book of Common Order of the Church of Scotland (St Andrew Press, 1994)

The Carmina Gadelica, collected by Alexander Carmichael (Floris Books, 1994)

The Divine Office ©1974 The hierarchies of Australia, England and Wales, and Ireland (Collins, 1987)

The Daily Office and Theotokia of the Coptic Church, De Lacey O'Leary (Simpkin, Marshall, Kent & Co. Ltd, London, 1911)

The Glenstal Book of Prayer (The Columba Press, 2001)

The Iona Community Worship Book (Wild Goose Publications, 1992)

The Revised Common Lectionary

The Rhythm of Life: Celtic Daily Prayer, David Adam (Triangle, 1996)

Worshipping Ecumenically, Per Harling, ed. (World Council of Churches Publications, Geneva)

The Community of Aidan and Hilda

Prayer Rhythms is the worship book of The Community of Aidan and Hilda. This is a dispersed body of Christians who seek to cradle contemporary expressions of Christian spirituality and monastic church, and to heal wounded lands. In the earthing of that commitment members draw inspiration from Celtic saints such as Aidan and Hilda.

Members follow a way of life, with a soul-friend, based on a rhythm of prayer, work, re-creation, study and out-reach. They seek to weave together the separated strands of Christianity.

The Community has members and groups in four continents and advisers from different Church streams. In the UK and Ireland it is an Associate Body of Churches Together in Britain and Ireland.

Its UK office and retreat house is The Open Gate, The Holy Island of Lindisfarne, Berwick-upon-Tweed TD15 2SD; aidan@theopengate.ndo.co.uk

Its website is www.aidan.org.uk. The US website is www.aidantrust.org

The story of the Community and a commentary on its Way of Life is published by Kevin Mayhew Ltd as *A Pilgrim Way*.